Restoring Dominion:

A Prophetic Look at Ezra and Nehemiah

Barbara Lodge HAYNES.

PRESS

www.xulonpress.com

Contents

Preface

Where do I begin? I began to reread the book of Ezra, as I have done many times, and as I read, I began to see it as I had never seen it before. I actually did a double take—was I seeing what I thought I was seeing?

The Lord put it in my heart as I read that the book of Ezra is a picture of the history of the restoration of the church in the twentieth century. As I read it, a panorama unfolded before me. I began to read history books about the origins of the Pentecostal movement, the Latter Rain movement, and the Jesus movement—the three major movements of the last century. I was amazed at the parallels I began to see.

After I saw these things, I once again read my way through the book of Ezra. This time I realized that there was a second parallel: the resurrection of the state of Israel. There it was! The parallels between the restoration books, the church, and Israel were remarkable.

As I began to fit the pieces of this puzzle together, I saw an incredible picture of the past one hundred years of church restoration. This restoration included the restoration of the *charismata* (the gifts of the Holy Spirit), the reality of the power of God among us, and the restoration of the fivefold ministries.

But the job isn't finished yet, is it? I began to seek the Lord again, and He spoke to me that the book of Nehemiah, which *was* the next wave of restoration when it occurred in the past history of Jerusalem, is also the next wave of restoration for both the church and Israel today.

So this book is a history book, in a sense. Part of this book tells the story of the past one hundred years. Part of it explains what is happening now. And finally, part of it tells the exciting future of the church, which is rapidly coming into fruition.

It is so exciting to see God's panoramic picture of His will for His people—both Jew and Christian. Both are, in a sense, His "elect." It makes sense, then, that God would etch into His Word His plans for His elect. Here is a sketch of what God showed me as I read His Word and listened to His voice.

Introduction

The world is in turmoil. We cannot listen to the radio or check out the news on the Internet or television without news of some new, dire catastrophe. It is enough to cause the most courageous of us to succumb to fear. But this is not what God wants for His people. In fact, not only does He want us to understand our times, but He also wants us to be victorious in these times. With that in mind, this book is intended to help us all understand the times in which we live.

Paul said, "But you, brothers, are not in darkness, so that this day should surprise you like a thief" (1 Thess. 5:4). God intended for us to know what is going to happen. In this hour of history, the Lord wants us to be prepared for what is coming so that in the times of persecution we will stand strong. We must not fear in this hour. We must rejoice! We must realize who we are in Christ, take our places in the overcoming army of the most high God, and fight the good fight, knowing God's plan is our birthright. It will help us to stand strong.

I recently heard an interesting story about the son of a prominent contemporary minister. This minister's son received many prophetic words that told him one day he would be the president of the United States. He made a conscious decision to attend law school based on these prophetic words. He subsequently joined the armed services and is currently an attorney with the Judge Advocate General's office. Recently he received another prophetic word similar to the first ones (this prophet had no idea that these words had been given earlier). This young man has based his entire life's plan on these prophetic words. He is preparing for what God has called him to do. He has a vision and understands his purpose in God's plan, and he is acting in accordance with that vision. He also is honoring the prophetic word, which gave him his vision. He has set his face like flint to accomplish God's will for his life.

This is the kind of hour in which we live: an hour that we must honor God's prophetic word and work according to the vision God has for each of us. God is laying out His prophetic plan for His church so that we may plan accordingly. If we fail to hear His prophetic plan, we will not only see our nation fall, but we will also, I believe, foil the plan of God for our generation and the generations to come.

In Acts 13:36, we read, "David had served God's purpose in his own generation." Are we willing to serve God's purpose for this generation? Or will we simply give up when pressure is applied by a culture that has embraced evil as good and good as evil? God is giving us a choice—He will not force His will on us. But His heart is hopeful that we will love Him like He has loved us. He has loved us with His best, with everything He has. Can we give Him any less than everything we have?

Jesus gave us a specific instruction before He went to heaven. He said, "Occupy till I come" (Luke 19:13, KJV). In military terms, occupation means to take charge of an area and, as necessary, to keep order by force. We are to occupy. We cannot simply shrug our shoulders and hunker down until Jesus comes to rescue us from this mess. He is coming for a *glorious church,* and there is nothing glorious about defeat. No, we must take back what the enemy has stolen. We do have the power. We do have the right. We do have the mandate. "The kingdom of God suffereth violence, and the violent take it by force" (Matt. 11:12, KJV).

God, in this hour, is looking for a church that understands spiritual warfare. He is looking for people who will humble themselves and pray and seek His face so that He can hear from heaven and heal their land. He is looking for someone to stand in the gap and build a hedge on behalf of the land so that He will not have to destroy it. Will He find such a person? Will He find such a people?

With all of these things in mind, I would like to share with you what God has shown me regarding what has been, what is now, and what is coming for the church in the United States and perhaps the world.

Chapter 1

The Plan of Restoration

From the time of the first return from Babylon to the time of the completion of the wall of Jerusalem, nearly one hundred years transpired. Why did it take so long? Because of continual attacks of the enemy, weariness of the people, and, well, the timing of God.

Frankly, I think God deliberately allowed this length of time so that we in this day would discover His plan for this hour hidden in the pages of the books of the restoration. God's pattern of restoration is deliberate. There are no mistakes in His design. It is perfect!

God designed restoration to take place in waves. It is as if the ebb and flow must take place so that when the time comes for complete restoration, there will be a great whoosh of His power to give birth all at once!

Jesus said it would be like a woman giving birth. When a woman begins to go into labor, sometimes she does not at first realize that the pains she is experiencing really *are* labor pains. She may feel strange aches in her back or cramps in her lower abdomen. Thinking she is just tired, she may ignore them at first.

As the pains increase in intensity and frequency, she begins to realize this is really it! She goes to the hospital, where she is connected to a monitor to watch the baby's heart rhythm. She is not allowed to eat or drink anything. The pains become more intense, and she begins to get hungry, tired, and irritable. The pains continue to grow in intensity and become more frequent until they are almost on top of each other. This, of course, takes hours. By the time she reaches the transition stage of the birth, she is already tired and in a lot of pain. She may be perspiring heavily. The pain of childbirth is upon her, but she has yet to push the infant out of her body.

Transition is the hardest part of childbirth. If she pushes too soon, the infant may die. If she doesn't push soon enough, she may die. If her body is not ready, she could tear the birth canal, causing trauma and more pain. She must be assisted at this point. She cannot do this alone. Her doctor or midwife helps her to deliver her baby by telling her when to push, how long to push, and when to stop. She is in pain. She is fatigued. She is desperate to give birth and yet is afraid of all the pain. What she really wants is for it to be over with.

I believe that in this hour we are this woman in transition. We are fatigued. We are in pain. We don't know when to push, how long to push, or how hard to push. We are desperate to give birth to the kingdom of God on this earth, but we are in need of a coach to tell us what to do.

God's coach for us is the mature fivefold ministry. Our recognition of those apostles, prophets, teachers, pastors, and evangelists that God has raised up is imperative. They are the midwives. We must allow them to do their jobs in this hour. We must accept their coaching so that we can birth the massive restoration in this hour that God has carefully planned.

With that in mind, let us now see the elaborate plan that God has been working on for the past one hundred years. We will look at the restoration books chapter by chapter and see the beautiful tapestry of God's plan.

The Book of Ezra

Chapter 2

The First Wave

In Ezra we will see three waves of restoration as the story unfolds. Each wave represents a paradigm shift in the way the church operates. The first question is, did God have a church before the twentieth century? The obvious answer is yes. The second question is, did God use the church as it existed before the twentieth century? Again, the answer is yes. So why change? What possible purpose would it serve to change the way the church had been doing things for eighteen hundred years?

God's purpose in the earth is to rule and reign with His church on this planet. His original purpose for man as stated in Genesis 1:28, is "be fruitful, multiply, and fill the earth and subdue it [with all its vast resources]; and have dominion over the fish of the sea, the birds of the air, and over every living creature that moves upon the earth" (AMP).

If God's intention was for us to have dominion over the earth, we have failed. There are a great many things that man does not rule over. Where we have ruled, we have in many cases ruined. We don't seem to understand the difference between dominion and domination.

Again, Jesus said, "Occupy till I come" (Luke 19:13, KJV). As the church, we have not occupied. We have failed at this. But why have we failed? Are we missing something? The obvious answer is yes. We are not even equal to the first-century church. This is why there must be restoration. We must fulfill the original intent. We must be the overcoming army that God intended for us to be. He is not coming for a feeble, ragtag bunch of losers. He is coming for a "glorious church, not having spot or wrinkle or any such thing" (Eph. 5:27, KJV). This is the purpose of restoration: that God can present to Himself such a church to be His bride and rule with Him.

For this reason, we cannot continue to think as we thought a hundred years ago or a thousand years ago. We must be restored to the fullness of gifting, fruit, and works with which God will empower us. This entails thinking differently. What is repentance, after all, except *changing your mind?*

In the book of Ezra, we read:

> In the first year of Cyrus king of Persia, in order to fulfill the word of the Lord spoken by Jeremiah, the Lord moved the heart of Cyrus king of Persia to make a proclamation throughout his realm and to put it in writing:

"This is what Cyrus king of Persia says:

" 'The Lord, the God of heaven has given me all the kingdoms of the earth and he has appointed me to build a temple for him at Jerusalem in Judah. Anyone of his people among us—may his God be with him, and let him go up to Jerusalem in Judah and build the temple of the Lord, the God of Israel, the God who is in Jerusalem. And the people of any place where survivors may now be living are to provide him with silver and gold, with goods and livestock, and with freewill offerings for the temple of God in Jerusalem.' "

—Ezra 1:1–4

The first return happened in approximately 538 BC. It was an incredible miracle. About seventy years before, the prophet Jeremiah had prophesied that the Jews would be in captivity for seventy years. The Jews knew their time of freedom was coming. Isaiah prophesied that a king named Cyrus would commission the rebuilding of the temple *175 years before it happened!* In Isaiah 44:28–45:1, God declared that *He* would set up a king named Cyrus who would defeat kings and rebuild the temple in Jerusalem. Can you imagine Daniel walking up to King Cyrus with his copy of the book of Isaiah the prophet and saying, "Hey, King Cyrus, look here! This was written about you 175 years ago"? That must have blown the king's mind!

So King Cyrus, seeing he had a divine commission to rebuild the temple, freed the captive Jews to return and begin work. But his declaration essentially said they could return but would have to pay their own way. And only a token of the Jews actually opted to return to Israel at that time. Only a chosen few actually decided to take the king's offer. They were the ones who were desperately hungry for God's presence and their way of life in God's chosen land.

With the statement of Cyrus, there were no qualifiers about who could go to Jerusalem. Everyone was invited. This invitation was extended to everyone who called himself a Jew. It was not limited to the priesthood, the elite, or the educated. Everyone could go. But only some *chose* to go. What did Jesus say? "Many are called, but few are chosen" (Matt. 22:14, KJV).

At the beginning of the twentieth century, God began to woo people to Himself through the restoration of the baptism of the Holy Spirit. It began slightly before 1900 with the Holiness movement. People began to seek God earnestly. It wasn't until people began to experience the actual baptism of the Holy Spirit with the evidence of speaking in tongues that the wave hit. And it hit only those who voluntarily sought it.

At first those who experienced this manifestation of the power of God were ostracized. Just as the first returning Jews had to pay their own way, those first saints in the restoration had to pay a price for the genuine fire of God. And just like the Jews who opted to return in the first wave, these saints who were seeking God began as a small band of believers.

God's invitation was to everyone. The incredible power that began to be poured out during that first wave is something we have not seen since. Creative miracles, such as whole arms and legs being re-created, occurred. Tumors fell off. The blind received sight. The deaf were healed—in groups!

Ezra 1:5–11 says:

> Then the family heads of Judah and Benjamin and the priests and Levites— *everyone whose heart God had moved*—prepared to go up and build the house of the Lord in Jerusalem. All their neighbors assisted them with articles of silver and gold, with goods and livestock, and with valuable gifts, in addition to all the freewill offerings. Moreover, King Cyrus brought out the articles belonging to the temple of the Lord, which Nebuchadnezzar had carried away from Jerusalem and had placed in the temple of his god. Cyrus king of Persia had them brought by Mithredath the treasurer, who counted them out to Sheshbazzar the prince of Judah.
>
> This was the inventory: gold dishes, 30; silver dishes, 1,000; silver pans, 29; gold bowls, 30; matching silver bowls, 410; other articles, 1,000. In all, there were 5,400 articles of gold and of silver. Sheshbazzar brought all these along when the exiles came up from Babylon to Jerusalem.

The first people who went were the heads of households of the three tribes of Judah, Benjamin, and Levi, which were the families of the king, the priest, and the favored son. God moved on their hearts. Did you get that? They did not go back just because of their arbitrary choice. *God moved on their hearts!* These were the people whose hearts *belonged to God, so He moved them to go.*

In the first wave of 1900, there were people who had been praying, fasting, and seeking God for revival. Many of the Holiness churches, such as the Church of God, had formed because of a passion to seek God for more. *Their hearts belonged to God.* When the fullness of time had come, God poured out His Spirit on these people who had been seeking Him.

It was also during this time that God chose to restore His manifest presence to the earth for the first time in nearly two thousand years. Reports from the Azusa Street revival describe the glory of God like smoke filling the meeting room, even oozing out into the street. Fire often appeared on the building—so much so that neighbors would call the fire department!

Also, the gifts were restored, just as the silver and gold vessels were restored to the temple. These articles of silver and gold were the tools used in the temple to perform the acts of worship prescribed in the Torah, or the Pentateuch, which are the first five books of the Bible. In the same way, the gifts (1 Cor. 12, Rom. 12, and Eph. 5) are tools for the church to use as acts of worship in service to the Lord. The restoration of the gifts to the church reempowered the church to do the work of the ministry. Without the gifts, the church had been unable to do what was normal Christianity according to first-century standards.

There were some 5,400 separate articles returned to the Jewish remnant. This is a picture of the vast variation of gifts in the lives of the saints. Each gift is unique and necessary to make the body whole and complete. Each person's gifting is a little bit different in keeping with each person's separate personality. But all are necessary to complete the work of the ministry.

In addition to the restoration of the Spirit of God and His giftings in the first wave, there was another first wave taking place in the early 1900s: the restoration of a pure language. Zephaniah wrote, "For then I will restore to the people a pure language, that they may call on the name of the Lord, to serve Him with one accord" (Jer. 3:9, NKJV).

When God restored the baptism of the Holy Spirit at the turn of the twentieth century, he restored a pure language of worship to the church: the gift of tongues. This is the pure language spoken by the Holy Spirit on behalf of the believer. This enabled the church to *call on the name of the Lord, to serve Him with one accord.*

But at this time, God was also raising up a small group of Jews who hungered for their homeland. During this time, God gave wisdom to one man, Eliezar Ben Yehuda, who made it his life's work to restore Hebrew as a modern spoken language. Never in the history of mankind had a dead language been resurrected. But despite the odds, a pure language was restored to the Jews. Hebrew became a spoken language after two thousand years of dormancy.

This timing was no coincidence. The restoration of the gift of tongues, the miraculous power of the Holy Spirit in the church, and the resurrection of the dead Hebrew language were the first part of the first wave of restoration begun at the turn of the twentieth century.

In Ezra 2, from verses 1–67, the people who arrived in the first wave of return are enumerated. The family names are listed in great detail. The reason for this is that in the tradition of Israel, a person could not be part of worship in the temple unless he could prove his lineage. Sometimes this genealogy may seem tedious, but the necessity of proving lineage was God's way of protecting the proof of the Messiah's lineage when He finally came. The Levites, too, had to prove lineage in order to serve in the courts of the temple.

Why is this important to us? Because it is also a picture of the fact that none of us may assume acceptance into the kingdom of God. We must have lineage; we must be part of the immediate family. In other words, we must be born again.

In the history of the restoration of the twentieth century, I believe relationship through salvation entered through the Holiness and the Pentecostal movements. This restoration of relationship and power took place from 1900 to the 1920s. For about twenty years, God began to restore true worship through those who had this relationship. He opened the door for ministers to restore His power and true depth of relationship with Him.

In verses 68–70, we see both the beginning of worship in the giving of freewill offerings and the beginning of setting things in order in Israel. The heads of the families "gave freewill offerings toward the rebuilding of the house of God on its site" (v. 68). The Levites, taking the lead, "settled in their own towns" (v. 70). They prioritized and set in order.

In the first twenty years of the twentieth century, we see God beginning to put into motion the ordering of the restoration. First came the restoration of the baptism of the Holy Spirit, and second was the beginning of the foundational churches of this new Pentecostal movement: the Pentecostal Church, the Assemblies of God, the Churches of God, the Foursquare Church, and others. These churches upset traditional church order by their free worship, the autonomy of their pastors, and the establishment of a plural hierarchy with no one person running the denomination. The movement of the Holy Spirit was paramount, and following His path was all that mattered.

In the Zionist movement, God moved on the hearts of the British government to publish the Balfour Declaration after World War I. This mandated a Jewish homeland. The Zionists slowly began to trickle into Palestine, very unobtrusively purchasing land there and beginning *kibbutzim* (communal farms). The seeds of a new homeland had been planted.

Unfortunately, the British reneged on their promise when it became evident that the Arabs in the area, who were sitting on massive oil reserves, did not want to share the land of Palestine, no matter how deserted it was. This false step by the British would later come back upon them. In Zechariah 2:8, we read, "Whoever touches you [Israel] touches the apple of his eye." When the British did not give Israel the homeland they had promised, the empire on which the sun never set literally fell apart within twenty-five years, and the great British Empire was no more.

Chapter 3

Restoration of True Worship

In Ezra 3:1–6, we see that after the people had moved back into their homes, the priest Jeshua and the prince Zerubbabel began to build an altar and sacrifice burnt offerings on it, even though the foundation of the temple had not yet been laid.

Do you recognize the name *Jeshua?* It is the name *Jesus* in Hebrew. It means, literally, "salvation." The name *Zerubbabel* literally means "from Babylon." It speaks of the fellowship of Jesus with those of us who were born in sin. It speaks of new, intimate fellowship, that we would be kings and priests along with Him.

The first feast celebrated in the restoration was the feast of Yom Kippur: The Day of Atonement, which comes roughly in September on the modern calendar. It is the most sacred day of the Jewish religious year. It occurs five days after the Feast of Trumpets (the Jewish New Year). Tradition holds that this day the penitent can receive forgiveness of all of their sins, if they have forgiven others. It also is considered a day in which God 'opens the Book of Remembrance' and writes the names of the forgiven, so that those who have been forgiven may go to heaven if they die.

It was also the only day that all sin could be repented of and be completely forgiven. It was the only day that the high priest could enter the Holy of Holies to sprinkle blood on the mercy seat to atone for the sins of the nation. It was the feast of repentance and forgiveness. In Jewish tradition, this season was the time when the gates of heaven were open and God would grant every request.

The priests did not want to waste another year waiting for the temple to be built; they wanted to atone for their sins and get right while the gates of heaven were open.

They offered sacrifice according to the Law—in obedience. The hunger that these two men, Jeshua and Zerubbabel, felt drove them to seek this kind of freedom from sin. For seventy years, they had been denied the opportunity to have their sins forgiven. They understood God's covenant. They did not even wait for the temple to be rebuilt; they built an altar and began the sacrifices.

Immediately following Yom Kippur was the Feast of Tabernacles (Succot). This was the most joyous, festive time of the year. The booths they built were similar to our tradition of Christmas trees; they decorated them with flowers, beads, and whatever was fun and cheerful. It was a time of celebration and dancing.

Their sins were forgiven, and they were clean. Now was their opportunity to tabernacle with God, to have personal fellowship with Him. It was a week-long celebration!

In the church, we also saw the beginning of worship in the Spirit. While the Holiness movement preceded Azusa, it was on Azusa Street that people began the practice of singing in a heavenly language. Not wanting to wait for formalities, the people of Azusa Street would worship as soon as they arrived and begin to praise God, sometimes for hours, and the *shekinah* glory of God would come. They would dance before God, unashamed. The joy they felt provoked them to share and pray with others, seeing the power of God move even before the preacher arrived. The power of God was so mighty and so evident that people a mile away would feel the conviction of God and begin to repent of their sins. People were healed in the street in front of the church.

In Ezra 3:7–9, the priests and people gave money to masons and carpenters to begin work on the temple. These workers immediately began obtaining logs from Lebanon and working with stone, carving it and cutting it to fit precisely. It took approximately two years for work to commence on the temple mount, the actual building of the foundation, but this preparation was necessary. The temple could not have been built without it.

No stonecutting tools could be used on the temple at the site, for no work of man took place in the house of God. It was God's house, and He would do the work. When Solomon built the first temple, he established this tradition, and it was not broken. So the men did all the cutting and hard work elsewhere, and then the stones were moved and laid at the site with no tool used when the walls were erected so that the temple would remain holy. When you consider this was all hand-hewed stone and hand-cut lumber, two years doesn't seem so long.

The Levites were appointed to supervise the work. This is a picture of the reestablishment of pastors as builders of the house of God, which is the church. This paradigm has been practiced for the past one hundred years.

Ezra 3:10–13 says:

> When the builders laid the foundation of the temple of the Lord, the priests in their vestments [a picture of those pastors] and with trumpets [a picture of the gifts of the Spirit] . . . with cymbals [again, the gifts], took their places to praise the Lord. . . . With praise and thanksgiving they sang to the Lord: "He is good; his love to Israel endures forever."
>
> And all the people gave a great shout of praise to the Lord, because the foundation of the house of the Lord was laid. But many of the older priests and Levites and family heads, who had seen the former temple, wept aloud when they saw the foundation of this temple being laid, while many others shouted for joy.
>
> No one could distinguish the sound of the shouts of joy from the sound of weeping,

because the people made so much noise. And
the sound was heard far away.

This is a picture of the church in the early twentieth century. There were essentially two factions:
those who remembered the past and those who saw
the future. Those who remembered the past wept
because they were feeling the pain of loss. Those who
saw the future rejoiced because of the incredible intimacy they were experiencing and the manifest presence of God in their midst. The rift, which continues
even now, is one that we must always guard against.
Will we cling to the past, or will we move on with the
cloud of His presence?

In a new paradigm, when the cloud of God moves
on, we can cry about what is lost or rejoice because
something new is coming. God is a God of infinite
creativity and variety. He gives us brand-new grace
every morning. He is able to be new and fresh. But
can we forget what lies behind and press on? Or are
we more interested in the comfortable: the rituals we
love, the songs we sing, the patterns we use?

Chapter 4

Trouble and Delays

After the foundation was laid again, the enemies of Judah came and offered to help. They lied, saying, "Let us help you build because, like you, we seek your God and have been sacrificing to him since the time of Esarhaddon king of Assyria, who brought us here" (Ezra 4:2).

This tactic is the first used to try to stop the people of the return: pretend to be sheep and infiltrate the flock. These people were eventually called Samaritans. They had formerly been Jews but had intermarried and in the process of generations had accepted the detestable practices of foreign gods. They may have thought of themselves as Jews, but their lifestyles were not faithful to the Torah. Zerubbabel and Jeshua and the rest of the heads of Israel answered them, "You have no part with us in building a temple to our God" (Ezra 4:3). Their answer was a direct one, refuting the claim. The spirit of compromise wanted to infiltrate the Jews, but the truth could not be denied. The Jews won the first round!

The first tactic of the enemy is usually geared to either deceiving or destroying the leadership. Because of this, the leadership confronts, head-on, the lies that the enemy is speaking. Speaking the truth is the first part of spiritual warfare. The gift used is discernment: recognizing the difference between true sheep and false ones. But there were not enough people who would fight for the will of God that the enemy would turn tail and run. The leaders stood up to this first attack. But as the first attack was focused on the leadership, the second one focused on the people.

The second tactic is discouragement: "Then the people around them set out to discourage the people of Judah and make them afraid to go on building. They hired counselors to work against them" (Ezra 4:4–5).

This was a devious attack on the people of God by the enemies of God. They hired "counselors" — read that "lobbyists" — to go to the royal court and curry favor with the king and the governors to stop the people of God. Their goal was to stop the people of God and the purposes of God. They were looking for decisions from the powers of the day to validate their own agenda and make the legal work of the Jews look like illegal activity. By successfully lobbying against the Jews, the enemies of God did just that. This did put fear into the people in general, which kept them from working on the restoration of the temple.

This was also the season that Xerxes became king of the empire. Perhaps you recall the story of Esther. In it there were evil men, enemies of Israel, who sought to exterminate the Jews. This season in Jerusalem would have been a terrifying season. Imagine how the Jews must have felt, knowing that the winds of change had blown so far that not only had they fallen out of favor after the death of Cyrus but now were to be hunted and exterminated! This season seemed to be the doom of the restoration.

A new king had ascended the throne, so the enemies of God knew when to make their move. The old king, Cyrus, knew he had issued an edict allowing the Jews to return and rebuild the temple. Even though the lobbyists may have had some reasonable arguments against building the temple, the laws of the Medes and Persians could not be repealed. But a new king might not be aware of a law enacted before he became king.

Xerxes did nothing to encourage the work of the temple (there is not much written about him, and his reign was a short one). Then Artaxerxes ascended to the throne. With the ascension of this new king, Artaxerxes, the third tactic was used: half-truths and outright lies, trumped-up charges and dirty politics. In Ezra 4:12–16, we read a letter from the politicians in the Trans-Euphrates area who hated the Israelites and wanted them stopped. Following are excerpts from this letter, beginning in verse 13:

> If this city [Jerusalem] is built and its walls are restored, no more taxes, tribute or duty will be

paid, and the royal revenues will suffer. . . . It is not proper for us to see the king dishonored. . . . a place of rebellion from ancient times. That is why this city was destroyed. . . . If this city is built . . . you will be left with nothing.

King Artaxerxes issued an order: "Now issue an order to these men to stop work, so that this city will not be rebuilt until I so order" (Ezra 4:21). Notice that the king was concerned about the city being rebuilt. But they weren't rebuilding the city; they were rebuilding the temple. The king had been manipulated into believing these Jews were a bunch of rebels bent on the destruction of Medo-Persia. The government based its policy on a lie!

While God spared the Jews from extermination through the intercession of the little girl Esther, the Jews of Jerusalem were completely discouraged. In all fairness, it would be easy to look with the eyes of the flesh and see why they stopped building and didn't fight. They had become afraid for their lives and did not pursue God or His will. They simply stopped building.

This tactic was successful in stopping the building of the temple for *sixteen years*. The Jews gave up. They settled for a foundation slab for sixteen years. They went to their homes and did nothing to establish God's glory in the earth. Did they have a right to build the temple? Yes! Remember that the laws of Medo-Persia could not be repealed. All they had to do was to appeal to Artaxerxes to search the records for Cyrus's edict. But they did nothing.

The period of history from approximately 1930 to post–World War II (1946) was a time of stagnation in the church. Not only were there no great moves of God, but there was also a time of (at first) great carnality in the culture, which the church did not confront. Because the church failed to act in God's will as a body, the world fell first into the Great Depression and then into a devastating world war.

During the 1920s, people like Aimee Semple McPherson, Billy Sunday, and Charles S. Price continued to hold revival meetings, but by 1930 there was a distinct decline in interest among nonbelievers. The Pentecostal movement slowed and became irrelevant to society on the whole. Many of the great preachers of the movement were declining in age and popularity. God never leaves His church without a lamp, but this lamp had clearly dimmed. For about seventeen years (from 1930–1947), not much happened, really nothing to grab the attention of society at large. The church, full of power, retreated into its own home, ignoring the rebuilding that society needed.

It was during this period that the German school of "higher criticism," a movement that essentially discredited the Bible as the Word of God, was bearing the fruit of its heresy. The part of what is loosely known as liberal Christianity seemed to have more sway over society than those who were true worshipers of Christ. The real church did not fight for truth in society at large. Because of this, it lost influence.

During this period of about seventeen years, the Lord always had His people. But they retreated into the church. During this time, there were pockets of revival, with Kathryn Kuhlman and some others holding scattered revivals. None, however, impacted the culture. None of them changed the status quo. It seemed that the church had given up and become ineffective in society.

In Israel the British Mandate had stalled out. The British failed to establish the promised homeland for the Jews in Palestine. This fatal mistake caused the death of untold millions of Jews who could not escape from Europe when Adolph Hitler rose to power. This period from 1933 to 1945 proved to be one of the most horrific in modern history. The British did not honor God's people, and the result of their inaction was mass genocide of God's people. Not only did six million Jews die, but another three million Christians were also murdered, many of whom were trying to help the Jews escape the holocaust.

Because of Great Britain's failure to honor the Jews, Great Britain lost its place and power. The British Empire, on which it was said the sun never set because of its worldwide extent, fell apart completely by the end of 1948. As Genesis 12:3 says, "I will bless those who bless you and I will curse those who curse you." God will not honor a nation who turns its back on His people. Interestingly, just as Artaxerxes died after he issued the edict to stop the Jews from building the temple, so the British Empire disintegrated after breaking its promise to Israel.

It was not until after World War II, when the entire world saw what Hitler had done to the Jews, that the world was shamed into providing a homeland for them. The British kept order during the transition. Ironically, the solution was called the "two-state solution," with Israel being one state and what is now Jordan being the other state. Isn't it odd that we've forgotten that original two-state solution and that the world is now seeking another one?

Through all of this, the enemy foolishly thought he had won the war. But regardless of how some battles go, God always wins. He knows that when death is completed, resurrection is coming.

Chapter 5

The Prophets Speak

Words are powerful. Physicists are now telling us that the universe is made of sound particles. In these days of quantum physics, it has been discovered that the universe is made of a minuscule thing called a quark. So what is a quark? Would you believe that it is *sound?* The Bible says that God "upholds all things by *the word of His power"* (Heb. 1:3, NKJV, emphasis added). It also says, "The worlds were framed by the word of God" (Heb. 11:3, NKJV). Even science confirms the power of God's words!

Before God moves, He always speaks. How does He speak? Through His prophets! The words He speaks through His prophets are so powerful that they change the course of history.

Ezra 5:1–2 says:

Now Haggai the prophet and Zechariah the prophet, a descendant of Iddo, prophesied to the Jews in Judah and Jerusalem in the name of the God of Israel, who was over them. Then Zerubbabel son of Shealtiel and Jeshua, son of Jozadak set to work to rebuild the house of God in Jerusalem. And the prophets of God were with them, helping them.

You can know a real prophet by the effect he has. Of course we know that a prophet is known by the accuracy of his words. However, only the Spirit of God in the words spoken could inspire this kind of turnaround after sixteen years of inactivity.

It is a testimony to the power of the spoken word of God that as soon as the prophets had spoken, the two leaders rose up and began to work. There had been no change in their outward circumstances. Their enemies were still empowered to stop them. There had been no edict from the king. They were taking a huge risk in light of their situation. But they honored the words of the prophets.

So what did these prophets speak? We are going to take a side trip into the books of Haggai and Zechariah to see what got the people back to work in the face of legal troubles and persecution.

Prophets are interesting people. Prophets don't see things as other people do. In fact, if you have ever known someone who has prophetic leanings, you know that he or she seems to get revelation from a bowl of fruit salad! Prophets seem to see everything but what is happening in front of them. And when they *do* see what's happening in front of them, they seem to look past it into motives no one else seems to see.

When prophets look into the future, they seem to see faraway things as if those things were very near. I remember as a child going to Colorado and climbing (by car) to the top of a very high mountain. We were above the tree line at the Great Divide, and we could see for miles and miles. Mountain peaks were piercing the fluffy clouds below us, and those peaks could be viewed far off into the blue-gray distance. At such a far distance, we couldn't tell which mountain was the nearer mountain and which one might be miles further on. They were all gray-blue peaks.

That is what it is like in the prophetic vision. Prophets see the peaks, many large mountains, blending together in the distance. Which one is first? Which one is last? It is hard to tell, but prophets are only aware that the mountains are there and that they can see them. So in writing the vision they are seeing, they can only write what they see; and that sight, as the apostle Paul says, is only partial, "through a glass, darkly" (1 Cor. 13:12, KJV).

As we look at this prophetic vision of Haggai and Zechariah, keep this in mind. They saw the mountain range in all its blue-gray splendor. Their concept of the timing might have been a little skewed, because to a prophet the vision is always for now. They could see what they could see, and distinguishing the exact time of what they were seeing was in the gray-blue distance.

We will first look at the words of Haggai, then Zechariah. When we have a handle on these books, we will understand God's incredible love for His people and the passion God has to accomplish His plan in the earth.

Chapter 6

Haggai Speaks

Haggai the prophet had no lineage. In Jewish custom, a family line was all important, but Haggai had none. He was simply known as "Haggai the prophet." The fact that he was taken seriously, being without pedigree, speaks of the power of the word of God in his mouth. No other recognition is needed for him. Both Zerubbabel and Jeshua knew that what he was saying came from the throne of God:

> This is what the Lord Almighty says: "These people say, 'The time has not yet come for the Lord's house to be built.'"
>
> —Haggai 1:2

Have you ever heard that excuse, "It must not be God's timing"? How many times have we used that one ourselves? These people had been procrastinating for some sixteen years by this point. They took their stuff and went to their own homes, shrugging their shoulders and saying, "Oh well, we tried." The fact is, when things get rough, we frequently give up.

Haggai looked directly at these people, including the leaders, and confronted this attitude:

> "Is it a time for you yourselves to be living in your paneled houses while this house remains a ruin? . . . Give careful thought to your ways. You have planted much and harvested little. You eat, but never have enough. You drink, but never have your fill. You put on clothes, but are not warm. You earn wages, only to put them in a purse with holes in it. . . . Give careful thought to your ways. Go up into the mountains and bring down timber and build the house so that I may take pleasure in it and be honored," says the Lord.
>
> —Haggai 1:3–8

God is saying, "Where are your priorities?" So many times we simply give up and over time completely forget what we set out to do. If we do this about carnal things, how much easier is it to forget why we are here and what our mission is on this earth? Remember, this was sixteen years after they built the foundation. So for sixteen years, they had been worshiping on a parking lot—never getting around to building the church! Did they kind of forget about it? Maybe they didn't notice there was no building?

John Lennon said, "Life is what happens when you're making other plans." So what happened to the people of Israel? *Life!* They had given up and decided it just wasn't going to happen right now. Perhaps after seventy years of captivity, they were so accustomed to disappointment that they just gave in to it as soon as it came along.

God is saying, "Pay attention!" The lack they suffered was caused by their own inaction. When they did nothing, they became ingrown and self-centered. They began to put themselves and their needs before the worship that God deserves. They ignored the kingdom of God and began to build their own houses, lives, and families, not understanding that it is *God* who gives increase.

The consequences of selfishness are poverty, drought, and lack: "The heavens have withheld their dew and the earth its crops" (v. 10). When a nation ignores God, there are national consequences. The whole nation of Israel was suffering because they had stopped worshiping God!

In verse 12, we see that repentance started with the leadership. Zerubbabel and Jeshua, then "the whole remnant of the people," went back to work. They received the word of the Lord and realized, despite their poverty and lack, that if they didn't start building the temple of God, their lot would never improve.

Then just four simple words from the prophet made them willing to do whatever it took to complete the work: "I am with you" (v. 13). If God is with you, you have the majority. It is recorded, "So the Lord stirred up the spirit of Zerubbabel . . . and Jeshua . . . and of the whole remnant" (v. 14). This process took only three weeks, and the work was resumed.

About one month later around Yom Kippur, when all the Jews were present on the temple site and crying out to God, the word came to Haggai again: "Who of you is left who saw this house in its former glory? How does it look to you now? Does it not seem to you like nothing? But now be strong . . . and work . . . for I am with you. . . . This is what I covenanted with you when you came out of Egypt and my Spirit remains among you. Do not fear" (Hag. 2:3–5).

Haggai went on to describe a great shaking that would come. This shaking would occur during the messianic age. He began to see afar off, to the time when God would shake all nations, the heavens, and the earth. Then he declared a thing that was true then and has a meaning for the future as well:

AROUND YOM KIPPUR

"The silver is mine and the gold is mine," declares the Lord Almighty. "The glory of this present house will be greater than the glory of the former house . . . and in this place I will grant peace."

—Haggai 2:8–9

All of the riches of this world belong to God. This is as true now as it was in the days of Zerubbabel. And the promise of the greater glory still pertains to the kingdom of God. God never goes back. He always presses forward. He moves us from glory to glory. But this also requires something of us: putting the kingdom of God first and never forgetting that God is our first priority.

About two months after this Yom Kippur message from God, Haggai received another word. God reminded the priests and the people that because of their procrastination with rebuilding the temple, every offering they gave and every sacrifice they made was defiled. They were defiled because the people lacked faith—they didn't trust that God would make a way for them to build. They simply gave up. But because they were now restoring the temple, God declared, "From this day on, I will bless you."

What a promise! Up until this time, for well over ten years, they had suffered lack. In the natural, it didn't seem like anything had changed, but God was so delighted with their repentant hearts that He spoke a blessing on them. At this point, they had been building again for about three months—just ninety days. But they were now stirred up; they knew what God wanted, and they were going after it. Did you know that is all God wants? He's not after the performance—He is looking at our *hearts*. The work is only the evidence that our hearts are running after Him.

The final portion of Haggai is a personal prophecy for Zerubbabel. Haggai saw into the future again:

> Tell Zerubbabel governor of Judah that I will shake the heavens and the earth. I will overturn royal thrones and shatter the power of foreign kingdoms. I will overthrow chariots and their drivers; horses and their riders will fall, each by the sword of his brother.

> "On that day," declares the Lord Almighty,
> "I will take you my servant Zerubbabel son
> of Shealtiel," declares the Lord, "and I will
> make you like a signet ring, for I have chosen
> you," declares the Lord Almighty.
> —Haggai 2:20–23

What does this mean? Haggai was again seeing the future, but at two different points of the future. He was again seeing the shaking of nations, the defeat of worldly kingdoms at the end of days. But he was also seeing the Messiah, who was going to do this.

So what did that mean to Zerubbabel, who would not be present to see either of those events? There are two meanings: a contemporary one and a future one. First, God promised that Zerubabbel would be a signet ring, which signifies he would be able to write his own ticket with the king at present. His enemies would be defeated in their attempts to thwart his progress.

But the second meaning is the most wonderful gift of all. God was saying that because of Zerubbabel's willingness to lead these people to build His temple at a time when it could cost him his life, the line of the Messiah would come from him! He is named in the lineage of Jesus in Matthew 1 and Luke 3.

Chapter 7

Zechariah Speaks

Remember what I said about the blue-gray mountain peaks? If this holds true for anyone, it holds true for Zechariah.

By the time Zechariah received the revelation from God, Haggai had already delivered much of what he'd had to say. While Haggai received many words from the Lord, Zechariah was a seer. He had many visions that had multiple meanings, the depths of which are still being explored. The book of Zechariah also includes visions and prophetic revelations that God gave him over the course of the rest of his life; it was not all pertinent to the restoration of Jerusalem.

Two months after Haggai had brought forth a word of reproof to the remnant, Zechariah spoke these words:

> The Lord was very angry with our forefathers. Therefore tell the people:

This is what the Lord Almighty says:
"Return to me," declares the Lord Almighty.
. . . Do not be like your forefathers, to whom
the earlier prophets proclaimed: This is what
the Lord Almighty says: "Turn from your evil
practices." But they would not listen or pay
attention to me, declares the Lord. Where are
your forefathers now? And the prophets, do
they live forever? But did not my words and
my decrees, which I commanded my servants
the prophets, overtake your forefathers?

Then they repented and said, "The Lord
Almighty has done to us what our ways and
practices deserve, just as he determined to
do."

—Zechariah 1:2–6

What Zechariah was saying was that God contended with His people over and over again through the prophets, but they were stubborn and would not listen. Both the prophets and the people who ignored them were dead, but the word of the Lord, which was alive, bore the fruit God said it would bear: the kingdom of Israel fell because of their own sins. His Word always accomplishes that for which it is sent.

So the question Zechariah asked was, "Are you going to be smarter than your ancestors?" Their ancestors repented after the fact. If we repent early, we don't have to reap the consequences. If we wait and dawdle, we will feel the full wrath of our rebellion.

These are the words that pricked the hearts of the remnant. Both Zerubbabel and Jeshua were sensitive to the word of the Lord. Their response was a wholehearted repentance and return to the work of the temple. Because the leaders were sensitive to the word of the Lord, the people also responded.

But Zechariah saw so much. The visions he saw were so vast and meaningful; God showed him not only the times in which he lived but also the times of the Messiah Himself. And finally, God showed him the time of the end and what God would do in that time.

While the text doesn't say much about Zechariah's background, there is a good chance that he had lived in either Babylon or Susa and returned to Jerusalem with the first return. It is probable that he had read the book of Daniel. Imagine, if you will, that Zechariah read or at least knew of Daniel 9, where Daniel discussed the "seventy sevens." He knew that when the rebuilding of the temple began, the countdown to Messiah would also begin. As we read, his anticipation of Messiah is almost palpable as he ponders how wonderful God is—and how precise.

With this in mind, we will briefly review some of Zechariah's visions. This will not be an exhaustive study, but rather a brief overview of what he saw in relation to our study of Ezra and Nehemiah.

Vision 1: The Man Among the Myrtle Trees

This vision was of a man among myrtle trees, riding a red horse. With him were other horses of different colors. The man instructed Zechariah that their purpose was to ride throughout the earth, and they found the people of the earth at peace and at rest (myrtle trees represent peace and rest). This man cried out to God on behalf of Israel.

God responded with this: "I am very jealous for Jerusalem and Zion, but I am very angry with the nations that feel secure. I was only a little angry, but they added to the calamity. Therefore . . . I will return to Jerusalem with mercy and there my house will be rebuilt" (Zech. 1:14–16). God's response was that He would return to Jerusalem. His love for His city and His mountain never stopped. Jerusalem was His city, and it would be rebuilt!

This vision has several meanings. In addition to the reference to the city of Jerusalem being restored in the time of Ezra and Nehemiah, it also refers to the restoration of Jerusalem to the Jews in 1967. It also refers to the spiritual city of God, the church, which would be restored in the last days so that the church could complete its mandate of dominion on the earth. This vision is for today!

Vision 2: The Four Horns

Zechariah then saw four horns and four craftsmen. They were declared to be the nations that caused Judah to be scattered. Perhaps these are similar to the four kingdoms that war against God's people, as mentioned in Daniel 2 and 7. The four craftsmen are the spiritual powers (angels) that came to throw down these "horns."

In other words, Zechariah saw something of the four great nations that came against Israel/Judah and that there were spiritual powers at work for Judah to war on their behalf against these nations.

While this vision had meaning regarding the four nations that came against Israel in ancient times, it also has meaning for today. God is not going to leave Israel defenseless in this time. He will go to battle for His nation, and the enemies of Israel will be defeated.

Vision 3: The Measuring Line

Zechariah saw a man with a measuring line. The man told him he was going to measure Jerusalem because it would be so big it would be like a city without walls. The man called the Jews out of the "land of the north" (Zech. 2:6). He called them to leave Babylon and declared that YHWH would judge those nations so that their slaves would plunder them.

While this vision and prophecy had connotations for the period of the return, this also has to do with the twentieth century. First of all, the "land of the north" could not really be about Babylon or Persia, because they were located east of Israel. The route back to Jerusalem would have taken them northeast of Israel; however, technically, they had lived east of it. Zechariah was seeing far into the future, to a day when the Jews would be mistreated by people to the north of Israel—Europe and Russia. God promised to bring judgment on these nations for the mistreatment of His people.

It is today when Jerusalem has become so big that it is "a city without walls" (v. 4). And God has promised that He "will be a wall around it . . . and I will be its glory within" (v. 5).

Zechariah went on to prophesy about the Messiah's coming: "For I am coming and I will live among you. Many nations will be joined with the Lord in that day and will become my people" (vv. 10–11). This is a promise to the Gentile church.

I believe that God will ultimately unite those from Israel who turn to Messiah with those Gentiles who have given themselves to Christ, making what Paul calls "one new man" (see Eph. 2:11–16). When this uniting takes place, Paul states it will cause such revival that it will be likened to resurrection from the dead!

Vision 4: Jeshua, the Priest

At this point, Zechariah's prophecies turn to predict much about the Messiah. Zechariah saw Jeshua, the high priest, and Satan accusing him. The angel said, "The Lord rebuke you, Satan" (Zech. 3:2). Jeshua's clothing changed from filthy rags to rich garments and a clean turban.

This first part of the prophecy pertains to Jeshua, the high priest. God would sanctify him. This also has meaning for us. We cannot sanctify ourselves. The blood of Jesus does this work; He alone can clothe us in righteousness.

The promise to the church at the time of post–World War II is also indicated. The turban represents the beginning of the renewing of the mind; that is, the restoration of teaching ministry to uncover depths in the Word of God and to begin to understand the vision of dominion.

This angel continued to talk about the righteous *branch* that would come and a seven-faceted stone with an inscription on it. The Lord promised to "remove the sin of this land in a single day" (v. 10). Of course, this is referring to the atonement of the Messiah. Later we will see that this also pertains to the Jews coming to know Messiah en masse in a single day.

Vision 5: The Lampstand and Olive Trees

Zechariah saw a menorah with an olive tree standing on either side of it. When he asked what it was, he was told, " 'Not by might nor by power, but by my Spirit,' says the Lord" (Zech. 4:6). Not exactly an answer to his question! But he was also told that Zerubbabel would complete what he had started: he would be allowed to complete the temple in his lifetime.

The seven lamps are the sight of the Spirit of God, who sees everything. The olive trees are "the two anointed to serve the Lord of all the earth" (v. 14). They represent several things, but for this study they are the church and Israel. These two people groups are the only people groups who give YHWH worship.

The time is coming, and soon, when the messianic Jews and the Gentile church will become the lampstands—the beacons—to this lost and dying world. But this will be accomplished by God's Spirit, not by our efforts.

Vision 6: The Flying Scroll/The Woman in a Basket

Zechariah saw a flying scroll, and he saw a woman in a basket who was carried to Babylon and left there. The scroll is a curse on all who use God's name falsely. The woman in the basket represents the false Babylonian system, both religious and governmental.

This is the start of judgment for the last days. There will be judgment on those who call themselves by the name of YHWH but are living contrary to His ways. There will also be judgment for the Jezebel systems of false religion and one-world government. This judgment comes on those in the worldly system — not on the people of God, who have given themselves to Him. Clearly, God will separate us from the worldly way of doing things — business as usual.

Vision 7: The Four Chariots and Jeshua's Crown

Again Zechariah saw horses, harnessed to four chariots and going forth in the earth. He also saw a crown given to Jeshua.

The horses, for our study, are instruments of change. They are going to find "rest" for the people of the next diaspora (after Jesus).

It is the crown for Jeshua that is significant; the word of prophecy says, "Here is the man whose name is the *branch*, and he will branch out . . . and build the temple of the Lord. It is he who will build the temple of the Lord, and he will be clothed with majesty and will sit and rule on his throne. And he will be a priest on his throne. And there will be harmony between the two" (Zech. 6:12–13, emphasis added).

Here is the actual name of the Messiah! Notice that Zechariah prophesied that Jeshua's *name* would be the branch, not Jeshua himself. It makes no sense that this high priest would be the king. No! What Zechariah was saying was that a man by the same name as Jeshua would become both king and priest: "there will be harmony between the two."

Then he prophesied that those who were far away would come and help to build the temple of the Lord. Zechariah again saw the messianic period when Gentiles would receive the good news of salvation and begin to build on the foundation of the Jews.

The next several chapters of Zechariah expound on the time of Messiah. In chapter 7, he rebukes the Jews for keeping fasts that are not of God. He then moves into very specific prophecies regarding Jesus' birth, life, and death.

We will pick up the thread of Zechariah's prophecies in chapter 12, verse 2. He declares, "I am going to make Jerusalem a cup that sends all the surrounding peoples reeling. . . . On that day, when all the nations of the earth are gathered against her, I will make Jerusalem an immoveable rock for all the nations. All who try to move it will injure themselves" (vv. 2–3).

This is, of course, what is coming. What God is restoring in Israel now will be defended by Him; the city without walls has YHWH for a wall! Zechariah goes on to say that all Jerusalem's enemies will be destroyed, but Jerusalem will be untouched. It will be on that day, when all the Jews see what God has done, that they will turn to Jesus: "They will look on me, the one they have pierced, and they will mourn for him as one mourns for an only child, and grieve bitterly for him as one grieves for a firstborn son" (v. 10).

On that day, God promises to remove impurity from Israel. But that will not be the last battle. There will still be more. God also promises to refine them like gold and silver.

Finally, Zechariah saw the day of the Lord, or the last battle. Jerusalem will be surrounded by her enemies for the last time. The city will be ransacked and the women raped. Then the Lord will come, and His feet will land on the Mount of Olives and split it in two. He will bring his holy ones with Him. Night and day will cease. And the Lord will be king over the whole earth.

This is a picture of His coming. We need to etch this into our minds so that we will focus on preparing for Him. No man knows the day or the hour, but we can know the season. Now is the season.

Chapter 8

The Resumption of Restoration

Approximately sixteen years had passed with no work on the temple. But with the word of the Lord through the prophets, the work resumed. While there had been considerable persecution during this interim, the leaders of Israel knew that God was speaking, and they were obedient.

In Ezra 5:2, we read, "Then Zerubbabel . . . and Jeshua . . . set to work to rebuild the house of God in Jerusalem. *And the prophets of God were with them, helping them*" (emphasis added). Those who boldly proclaimed the word were also in the trenches doing the work.

The regional governor still resisted them, but with a letter to the new king, Darius, they requested a search of the archives to prove they had not only the right but also the mandate to build this temple (see Ezra 5:3–6:5). In addition to this mandate, Darius ordered the governor—the very person who was challenging the Jews' right to restore the temple—to pay the bills! Ezra wrote these words of Darius:

> Moreover, I hereby decree what you are to do for these elders of the Jews in the construction of this house of God: The expenses of these men are to be fully paid out of the royal treasury, from the revenues of the Trans-Euphrates, so that the work will not stop. Whatever is needed—young bulls, rams, male lambs for burnt offerings to the God of heaven, and wheat, salt, wine and oil, as requested by the priests in Jerusalem—must be given them daily without fail, so that they may offer sacrifices pleasing to the God of heaven and pray for the well-being of the king and his sons.
>
> Furthermore, I decree that if anyone changes this edict, a beam is to be pulled from his house and he is to be . . . impaled on it.
>
> —Ezra 6:8–11

Wow! Not only did Darius declare that he would uphold the decree of Cyrus, but he also caused the government to pay for everything—the plan completely backfiring on the enemy!

The time was after World War II. The restoration of the fivefold ministry had begun. Pastors had always been present, and while there have been evangelists throughout the history of the church, the ministry of evangelist was being restored at this time. Just as

Haggai brought forth the word of the Lord to begin the work on the restoration of the temple, evangelists like Oral Roberts, T. L. Osborn, William Branham, and A. A. Allen began to be used of God to preach the gospel with signs following, and it was within this period that one of the greatest evangelists of the twentieth century, Billy Graham, began his ministry.

In fact, there was no shortage of major evangelists during this time. The restoration of evangelism as a part of the fivefold ministry was established. Now two parts were present: pastors and evangelists. These building blocks were the first in the restoration of biblical leadership of the great *ecclesia,* or the body of Christ. These building blocks were the first and most essential parts of the church. Without the evangelist being restored, there could be no Jesus movement, which would come later. Without pastors, where would the saved go to learn the ways of God? Where would they be safe? No, these two parts are literally the legs on which the body of Christ must stand.

As the Scripture indicates, there was another part of the body of Christ that needed to be in place for the other revivals to occur, and this was the financing of the work of God. It was during this period that the Full Gospel Businessmen's Fellowship International (FGBMFI) was formed. This piece of the puzzle reached out to the business community and had to be in place for the financing of great evangelistic crusades. The FGBMFI was a precursor to what God would do in the restoration of the marketplace ministry fifty years later. Thus the first parts of the restoration of the temple made without hands were restored.

At the end of World War II, the Jews were in devastation. Just as they'd suffered persecution for sixteen years at the time of the restoration in Ezra's day, so they suffered sixteen years of persecution by the Nazi regime in Europe. Six million of them were murdered in the concentration camps of Hitler. In addition, the survivors were debilitated by starvation; they were alone and homeless. All their belongings had been lost. Their families were either dead or torn apart. They had nowhere to go.

But God is faithful. Just as Ezekiel the prophet had seen the dry bones be resurrected (see Ezekiel 37), the people of Israel were given a homeland. The entire world, shamed by their inaction to help the Jews at the rise of Nazi Germany, consented to give the survivors a homeland in Palestine.

As Isaiah prophesied, "Can a country be born in a day or a nation be brought forth in a moment? Yet no sooner is Zion in labor than she gives birth to her children" (Isa. 66:8). On May 14, 1948, the state of Israel was born. God once again performed a miracle on behalf of His people!

The fact that this happened when it did—with the rise of the restoration of the first two parts of the five-fold ministry offices—is no coincidence. This restoration of Israel had to happen at this time because the birth of the two, Jew and Gentile (church), meant they would grow up together to become one new man in Messiah when maturity comes (we will discuss this more later).

The seed of the Jesus movement, which occurred twenty years later, started here with the planting of ministries that became the parents of the Jesus people. It was the great fathers in the Lord, like Bill Bright, Demos Shakarian, Oral Roberts, Kenneth Hagan, Sr., and Billy Graham, who helped give birth to the Jesus movement.

It was, likewise, the great fathers of Israel, men like David Ben-Gurion and Chaim Weizmann, who established the constitution of Israel. They were parents to the men who won the 1967 war, which paralleled the Jesus movement.

In Ezra 6:13–22, we see the completion of the temple. There are several points in this text that require a closer look.

First, we have to note that because three kings all decreed completion, the local pagan kings were required to help finance this task. With this financing in place, the remnant was able to complete the temple in record time.

Second, we see that they completed the temple in the month of Adar, the month in which Esther saved the Jews from annihilation. This event would have happened during this period, so the joy of the Jews from not only being saved from death but also having their beloved temple completed would have been overwhelming. The first feast, then, would have been Purim (the feast that celebrated their deliverance from Haman by Esther). Is it any wonder, then, that Ezra wrote, "The people . . . celebrated the dedication of the house of God with joy"?

Third, the Jews "installed the priests *in their divisions* and the Levites *in their groups* for service to God" (v. 18, emphasis added). When the Passover season arrived, the priests and Levites had purified themselves and were clean. Those who were part of the return ate with those who had "separated themselves from the unclean practices of their Gentile neighbors" (v. 21). In other words, as soon as the temple was completed, the leaders were set in order. If the leadership is not in God's order, nothing they do in God's name will be accomplished. Leadership must be built first before the rank and file can function properly.

Fourth and finally, Ezra writes, "For seven days they celebrated with joy the Feast of Unleavened Bread because the Lord had filled them with joy by changing the attitude of the king of Assyria, so that he assisted them in the work on the house of God" (v. 22). Why would they rejoice so much when they were fasting leaven? They had to eat matzos for a week and they were happy about it? Yes, because it was a remembrance of their escape from a wicked king who would not repent. But this time the pagan king did repent. In fact, not only did he leave them alone, but he actually helped them. This caused great joy.

During the approximately twenty-one years from 1946 to 1967, God was putting in order the leadership of His church. Many battles had to be won, not the least of which was breaking up the rocky ground of the religious rituals that had come to mean more to many church members than a fresh relationship with the living God. God had begun to move in ways that many churches were skeptical of — ways that changed the paradigm of traditional church. For example, the huge tent meetings of Oral Roberts saw mighty miracles, with the blind seeing, the deaf hearing, and the lame walking. T. L. Osborn also saw incredible creative miracles.

But there were many denominational churches who frowned on such "emotionalism." Of course, if you had received such a miracle, it would only make sense that you would feel pretty emotional! But God was working on these denominations, softening ground that had lain dormant for centuries.

Israel was at war from its inception. Surrounded by their enemies, they were required to fight for every inch of the small plot of land they had been given. The surrounding Muslim nations refused to acknowledge their existence. In the final mandate set forward by the United Nations, a two-state solution had been agreed upon. There was a small state given to Israel, which included the area of Tel Aviv to the Mediterranean coast. The Palestinians were given all of Jerusalem, Jericho, and the West Bank, including what is now Jordan (then called Trans-Jordan).

However, after the proclamation of the state of Israel, the surrounding Arab nations refused to allow the Palestinians permanent residence in these lands and instead imprisoned their own people in interment camps, which became permanent slums. The Arabs *wanted* these Palestinians angry. They *wanted* them to blame Israel for their plight, even though it had been inflicted by their own countrymen. This is the festering wound that Israel still faces today.

The wars the Israelis fought in 1948, 1952, and 1956 were, in a sense, preparation for the war of 1967. God was using these skirmishes to toughen them for the war that would return Jerusalem to them.

Chapter 9

Ezra Returns

U p to this point, Ezra was recording the history of what had happened before his arrival. Ezra was actually in the second wave of the returning remnant. About eighty years had passed since the first wave of returners arrived. More than fifty years passed from the end of chapter 6 to this new chapter 7. There were *decades* of silence.

During those decades, the temple worship resumed, and the remnant enjoyed the privilege of worshiping again according to the Torah. They enjoyed hearing the Word of God read aloud and hearing scribes and priests expound on it. They knew the forgiveness of God during the open-heaven times of Yom Kippur and Succot. They felt the protection of God while celebrating Passover. They once again knew the covering and covenant of the blood of the lambs. For fifty years before the arrival of Ezra and the new remnant, they enjoyed all these privileges of covenant with the almighty God, YHWH.

Ezra then arrived with a multitude of people who had been living in Babylon and in Persia. They were, of course, Jews. But their ways were foreign. They had not known temple worship. They arrived unwashed and still stinking from a long desert journey, clothed in Gentile clothing, having Gentile habits and mannerisms. These people had never known the previous temple. That old generation had died off. Instead, they only knew that they were Jews and that somehow they belonged here.

How would these people learn the ways of Jewish life? How would they fit into this concept of Torah, of being clean, of sacrificing a baby lamb they had taken into their homes for three days? Who would educate them?

Enter Ezra. At this time, Ezra was not a young man, but rather a highly educated teacher of the Torah. Perhaps he was some type of emissary in the Persian government who was sent to oversee these Israelites, since by this time Zerubbabel had died.

Ezra's pedigree was impeccable. He kept records of his family all the way back to Aaron. He had proof that he belonged in this temple. We read, "He was a teacher well versed in the Law of Moses, which the Lord the God of Israel had given" (Ezra 7:6).

As would have been the custom, Ezra could probably recite the Torah from heart in Hebrew. He would also have been fluent in the Persian language, since he had lived there all his life. So Ezra would have been versed in all the priestly rituals as well as familiar with the customs of the Persians. He was the one God would use to unify the old remnant with the new one, because he could communicate on either level. In addition to this quality, he was also zealous for God and for His Word.

This picture of Ezra and the returning remnant is a perfect picture of what God did in the Jesus movement. Jesus said, "Therefore every teacher of the law who has been instructed about the kingdom of heaven is like the owner of a house who brings out of his storeroom new treasures as well as old" (Matt. 13:52). Those great men of God whom God had raised up during the 1940s and 1950s were the ones that God used to teach the great "unwashed" of the Jesus movement.

So much happened in this movement that pertains to the restoration of the temple. Just as a multitude returned with Ezra, so a multitude of people came to know Jesus Christ in a real relationship. Just as the returning remnant were Jews who were completely socialized into Persian customs and manners, so we see that many denominations were completely turned upside down by the power of the Holy Spirit, with many new converts who had been raised in denominations coming to know Jesus for the first time. They had a lot of religious knowledge, but their mannerisms and customs were anything but biblical.

The Jesus movement started around 1967 and continued through approximately 1980. During this movement, God reached both the churched and the unchurched and turned Christianity completely around. It really began in several venues at once. In the Catholic Church, a revival broke out at Duquesne University in 1966 and spread like wildfire throughout the entire North American Catholic Church, with charismatic prayer meetings springing up in almost every parish. In 1963, Pope John XXIII had announced that the church would open up its windows and allow the Holy Spirit to blow through it. I wonder if he realized what that would mean!

Denominations that had been dormant for centuries awakened much in the same way. Many denominational leaders were bewildered. They had been taught that the gifts of the Holy Spirit had stopped with the apostles. But God had His way. Those who were willing to submit to the Holy Spirit saw their churches and ministries grow. Those who did not receive this move of God found themselves sidelined and their congregations dwindle.

Another part of this incredible move of God was the Jesus movement among the young people. Whenever God has a major move, the enemy attempts to corrupt it. Without belaboring the history of the enemy's counterfeits throughout the twentieth century, suffice it to say that during this period, sex, drugs, and rock and roll became the maxim of the day. Millions of teens and young adults were deceived into this depraved lifestyle. But God cannot be stopped. God began to pour out His spirit on these unwashed.

There was a small church in California that had only a hundred or so members. For reasons only God can know, young hippies began to show up for services at this little church. They were dirty, shoeless, and talked in ways that the aging congregation could not comprehend. This church was called Calvary Chapel, and its pastor was (and is) Chuck Smith. Pastor Smith didn't understand the why of it, but he knew that these young people needed the love of Jesus, and he accepted them. This began one of the greatest revivals in the history of the United States. From these humble beginnings came the Calvary Chapel movement and Maranatha music, both of which had a huge effect on the generation.

This was also the time that God restored the teacher to the fivefold ministry. This was the third part of this restoration of leadership. Just as Ezra had taught the remnant, so God restored the teacher to the body of Christ to create a firm foundation for what was to come. Men like Derek Prince, Watchman Nee, Winkie Pratney, and many others were brought forth to create a firm foundation for every Christian. Now *teachers* were restored as part of the fivefold ministry of Christ. Their teachings are for the people of God in general "to prepare God's people for works of service, so that the body of Christ may be built up" (Eph. 4:12). Taking the great unwashed and turning them into men and women of God necessitated the teacher's presence. Only the teacher with maturity and experience and who could rightly divide the Word of Truth could turn this motley crew into the army of God for the future move of God thirty years later.

Looking at the time of arrival, Ezra arrived in the fifth month (Ezra 7:8). This time is the beginning of the *latter rains* in the country of Israel. The fruit trees would have just been starting to blossom. The winter would have been coming to an end and spring starting. As Ezra and the remnant entered their homeland, they were probably greeted with some cool weather, but it would have soon been warming up, the latter rains starting and the fields showing the first signs of a haze of green. The trees would have been covered with buds. There would not yet have been fruit, but the anticipation of it would have been on everyone's minds.

This is a perfect picture of what happened in the 1960s and 1970s. The rain of God fell. The gifts of the Holy Spirit were in use everywhere. All were experiencing this incredible, rich flow of what God was doing. It felt like this was all of the "former and latter rains" that Joel had mentioned because this revival was so widespread. There was a great anticipation of the fruit to come. This was, in a sense, the first major contraction in the birth process.

In Israel, the restoration also continued in two different ways. In 1967, God miraculously restored Jerusalem to Israel. To understand the magnitude of this miracle, we need to consider the magnitude of the danger Israel was experiencing.

In 1967, Israel was roughly half the size it is today. At present, it is only the size of New Jersey, so at that time it was only slightly larger than Rhode Island. It was and is surrounded by its sworn enemies—people who intend to annihilate it. In 1967, these enemies joined together to declare war on this little nation, with the goal of utterly destroying it in what became known as the Six-Day War.

Three armed nations—Egypt, Syria, and Jordan—all descended on this little country. But Israel was able to defeat all three of them in just six days! Many reports of miraculous deliverance are known from that short war. For example, a small Israeli town that was unarmed came under attack by a battalion of armored tanks. Miraculously, the tanks were abandoned and their enemies went running and screaming, leaving their tanks behind! It seemed that swarms of bees attacked the tanks and swarmed their personnel, thus driving them out of the tanks.

The stories of miraculous deliverance are incredible. But the most incredible story is the taking of Mount Zion. In the process of taking Jerusalem (a stronghold of the Palestinians), the soldiers who came upon the mount wept. For the first time in two thousand years, the Jews owned Jerusalem and were able to touch the site of the temple. The "times of the Gentiles" had come to an end (see Luke 21:24).

In addition to the natural Israel's restoration, God began a restoration of the Jews to Himself, a movement called "Jews for Jesus." For the first time in nearly seventeen hundred years, Jesus showed Himself to be the Jewish Messiah to those of His people who sought Him. This restoration will be a key in future years as God unifies His church, both Jew and Gentile, into "one man." Again, we will discuss this later at greater depth.

In Ezra 7:11–28, Ezra copied the letter of Artaxerxes that gave him free passage to Jerusalem. In this letter, the king commissioned him to take offerings to Jerusalem to make sacrifices for him and the leaders of the nation. God gave such favor to Ezra! This was a pagan king, but the wisdom of Ezra was so superior to the other wise men that the king knew that he entrusted Ezra with the transport of all the remnant, the huge monetary offering for God, the animals for sacrifice, and the future appointment of judges and magistrates for all of Trans-Euphrates— "all who know the laws of your God" (v. 25).

But Ezra didn't take God's favor for granted. In chapter 8, after he'd taken a census of the returning remnant, he found he had no Levites with him. Concerned that there was no one to minister in the temple, Ezra sent for Levites of the correct lineage to go with him. God provided two families of priests who freely went with him.

In addition to this, Ezra proclaimed a fast because he did not want to ask the king for an armed guard, since he had already bragged that God would protect them. He didn't presume on God but rather called a fast to cry out to God for this protection. Ezra carefully planned and prepared. He made sure, not only that he had the right people, but also that those people were prepared spiritually and that God would go with them.

This careful planning is a picture of the preparation God made before He started the charismatic renewal. All had to be in place. God placed many good ministers who were prepared in the Word to carry forth the charismatic renewal within the walls of the church.

The gold and silver are pictures of the *charismata*, the gifts of the Spirit. The gold and silver were given to the Levites to protect. In the same way, the ministers who embraced this new move of God received the gifts first and then began to share them with their congregations. Millions received the baptism of the Holy Spirit during this period and found that they could have a real relationship with Jesus, not just dead religion. But the ministers who knew the Word were the key, just as Scripture refers to the scribe who knows about the kingdom of God as bringing forth things "both old and new" (Matt. 13:52).

In this same sense, after the Six-Day War in 1967, the Jews began earnest searches of their lineage to find pure Levitical priestly lines. The preparation for the restoration of the temple was in its infancy. Those who were found to be pure in lineage began to surface. In fact, there was a large group of men who had moved to a Mediterranean island over a thousand years ago with the purpose of preserving the Aaronic priesthood. These people could prove their pure lineage back to Aaron!

The doors began to open to allow Jews from all over the world to return to Israel so that all the prophecies that God would bring them back could be fulfilled.

All of these movements started in the 1960s. The end-time church had been birthed, and the covenant land had been rebirthed.

Chapter 10

Restoration of the Prophet

After the new remnant had arrived, rested, and settled all the gifts in the temple, the leaders came to Ezra and declared that "the people of Israel, including the priests and Levites, have not kept themselves separate from the neighboring peoples with their detestable practices . . . and the leaders and officials have led the way in this unfaithfulness" (Ezra 9:1–2).

Ezra called the people to repentance. He tore his garment and sat until evening. He cried out to God for mercy and led the way in the radical change that had to take place.

We know that "judgment must begin in the house of God" (1 Pet. 4:17). This passage is a transition from the charismatic movement to something new. It is an indication of the restoration of the prophet. As we have looked at the body of Christ, we have seen the two legs, the pastor and the evangelist. Now we have both the teacher and the prophet, the two arms of this body.

A prophet's purpose is to see what's coming and to tell others about it. The restoration of the office of prophet in the body of Christ marked four-fifths of the fivefold ministry and began to occur in the 1980s. Recognition of some men and women as prophets was a huge shift in the church's paradigm. It was, in a sense, easy to accept the first three ministries, because they had always been at least nominally present in the church. But how could we reconcile calling someone a prophet without sounding, well, outrageous?

Ezra, while a teacher in earlier chapters, now became the prophet to call the nation to repentance. In this chapter, Ezra is the perfect picture of the new covenant prophet. He heard the newly arrived leaders' plea for purity. He saw those who were already in the "church" (Jerusalem) who had compromised and allowed worldly ideas to corrupt them. He saw the religion without relationship. And he had a very healthy fear of God:

> When I heard this, I tore my tunic and cloak . . . and sat down appalled. *Then everyone who trembled at the words of the God of Israel gathered around me.*
> —Ezra 9:3–4, emphasis added

This is a picture of the first call to purity by the prophetic. In the 1980–1990 period, it seemed that not much changed. The momentum gained in the charismatic movement had continued, but slowed down. The prophetic began to call for purity of worship. The ministries of men like Bob Weiner, Bob Mumford, and many others were a call to purity and total commitment to Christ. Prophets like Dick Mills and Bill Hamon began to emerge. The vision that these men began to instill into the Body of Christ was the beginning of a new desire to see a whole, complete mature man. In other words, a hunger was birthed to see, not just the use of the gifts of the Holy Spirit, but a manifestation of the *fruit* of the Spirit, and a maturity within the Body of Christ that had not yet manifested.

This was the birth of this restoration. The growth of this prophetic ministry takes many years. One does not become a prophet overnight. This takes a lifetime of submitted growth, study, and, above all, humility. The school of God is in no hurry. It takes as long as it takes. But slowly the office of prophet began to develop.

In the rest of chapter 9, Ezra also showed himself to be a committed intercessor. This ministry of prophetic intercession, without which the church cannot survive, also began to emerge. The prophet is first an intercessor. Many of the recognized prophets of the 2000s started in these years as intercessors, weeping and crying out to God. The birth of such ministries as God's Generals, led by Cindy Jacobs, and International House of Prayer, led by Mike Bickle, started during this time

The first part of Ezra's prayer was to acknowledge his sin and the sin of his nation. He then began to acknowledge God's grace in the restoration of the remnant to Jerusalem. He also said, "He has given us a wall of protection in Judah and Jerusalem" (v. 9).

He continued:

> We have disregarded the commands you gave through your servants the prophets. . . . The land you are entering to possess is a land polluted by the corruption of its people. . . . Shall we again break your commands and intermarry with the peoples who commit such detestable practices? . . . Here we are before you in our guilt, though because of it not one of us can stand in your presence.
> —Ezra 9:10–15

Can you feel his anguish? He knew what sins God wanted cleansed from His land. He knew that compromise had caused his people to be banished from the land, and he understood that God would have been justified to allow them to die, but God had mercy in merely exiling them. And he also understood that God had kept His promise to restore them. How could they once again commit spiritual adultery with this great God, the lover of their souls?

This is always the heart of intercession. It begins with heartfelt anguish—a pain in the gut that makes the intercessor ache for restoration with God. It identifies with those people for whom the intercessor prays, and the intercessor finds himself taking on the spirit of repentance for them, crying to God to forgive and to have mercy. The intercessor yearns for others' restoration of intimacy with the One who is pure love and desperate to bring reconciliation.

This ministry of intercession and prayer, while always present in the body of Christ, is the very thing that God is using to bring all of us into a more intimate relationship with Him. Without intercession, there is no growth, no maturity, and no birth in the church. The intercessory ministry within the body of Christ at large, which began in the 1980s and continues to grow through today, is the key to seeing widespread repentance in the church and what will ultimately cause the great harvest to start. But this time it will not be one man. It will be a massive, churchwide intercessory effort. In the same way that a woman pushes with all that is in her to give birth to her baby, so the entire body of Christ must push with a great intercessory effort to give birth to the end-time army of God and the end-time harvest of souls.

Chapter 11

The Restoration
of the Apostle

This point is a transition point. We now move on to the present time in the body of Christ. You see, this is our present day. We will temporarily backtrack in the book of Nehemiah, but let's look now at Ezra and his sermon to see what God is doing now in His church, especially the western church.

As Ezra wept, prayed, and confessed, we see the following:

> A large crowd of Israelites . . . gathered around him. They too wept bitterly. Then Shecaniah . . . said to Ezra, "We have been unfaithful to our God by marrying foreign women."
>
> —Ezra 10:1–2

Ezra never had to preach. Because of his faithful, pure heart of intercession, the conviction of God fell on the people. They saw their compromise and realized its full implication. This one man, Shecaniah, made a suggestion:

> Now let us make a covenant before our God to send away all these women and their children. . . . Let it be done according to the Law. Rise up; this matter is in your hands. We will support you, so take courage and do it.
> —Ezra 10:3–4

Funny thing about a burden of intercession: If God gives you this burden and you pursue it faithfully, God will suddenly give you the responsibility to take action. It is at this point that we see the restoration of the apostolic ministry to the body of Christ. The apostolic is the ministry of the fivefold that "sets in order." It is the last of the fivefold to be restored. But without apostles, there will not be proper order. They are the church planters. They are the organizers, the inspirers, and the governors of the church. With the restoration of the ministry of apostle, the body of Christ is now whole.

In the church, this restoration began in the 1990s and continues to the present day. There are now, for the first time in almost two thousand years, people who genuinely move in apostolic ministry. We are no longer afraid to use the term *apostle* because we now understand that without people called to this ministry, we cannot complete the task of the great harvest, because the church planters and governors weren't there before.

The fivefold ministry was a gift from God "to prepare God's people for works of service, so that the body of Christ may be built up *until we all reach unity in the faith and the knowledge of the Son of God and become mature, attaining to the whole measure of the fullness of Christ"* (Eph. 4:12–13, emphasis added). Until we are complete, we need this gift of the fivefold ministry. God has been painfully and deliberately restoring it and has taken a century to meticulously perform this. Considering His care and nurturing in this, we must be equally as careful to respect it, to understand it, and to utilize the fivefold so that we can indeed reach maturity and attain to the full measure of Christ.

When Ezra rose up, he rose up with a new anointing, the apostolic, to set in order the plan of corporate repentance. This is huge. Ezra started his work with the priests and Levites and put them *under oath* to do what had been suggested (see verse 5).

This is the apostolic calling: set in order; do it now; do it this way. It is ordered according to God's will and done with a heart of godly compassion and brokenness. And after Ezra set in order, he withdrew and continued to fast and pray.

The life of an apostle is one of self-sacrifice and complete dependence on God. If God takes decades to raise up a prophet, it must be obvious He would do no less with the office of apostle. This office, being the last one to be revived, will be the one to set in order the true body of Christ now. This is God's current agenda.

The temple is now completed. The building is built. The treasure (the gifts) are wholly restored. We have seen all of the gifts of the Spirit (the *charismata*) for many years. Like children, we have played with those gifts in past moves of God. But the current move of God will start in the house of God—the church—to set in order and see maturity come to the people of God.

God is finished with compromise. He is starting with those in leadership, the Levites and priests. Those who wish to walk in the presence of YHWH must take an oath of purity. Then God will purify the people in His church:

> Then Ezra the priest stood up and said to them, "You have married foreign women, adding to Israel's guilt. Now make confession to the Lord the God of your fathers, and do his will. Separate yourselves from the peoples around you and from your foreign wives."
>
> —Ezra 10:10–11

Notice that these Israelites had not just lived around these people; they *married* them. This connotes they were intimately involved with them. They had children by these women. They had taken this sin into their bosoms. They had bonded with this sin. It had become a part of them. Compromise had become "family" and produced fruit.

What compromise do we see in our generation? I submit to you that we see much, even in "good" churches. We have tolerated everything from apostate worship to personal sin. We have winked at pastors who divorce their wives to marry their secretaries. We have not confronted sin in our midst: sexual sin, perversion, abortion, drugs, covetousness, greed, and much more.

It should be noted that most of the people repented; they turned their hearts to God and left their sins behind. All it took was the willingness of Ezra to confront. But there were a few who did not. I believe they are the picture of the apostate churches that have embraced sinful lifestyles and trampled the Word of God.

These people were not permitted to serve in the temple after this. They would have their way, but they would not have blessing, fellowship, or intimacy with God.

As Ezra draws to a close, we see that he lists all those who had married foreign women. These were the ones who repented, starting with Jeshua's sons (the former high priest with Zerubabbel). Jeshua, the one whom God had said He would name His Son after, had a son who had compromised. But this one turned again to serve God with all his heart. God is so merciful. When we repent, He is so proud of us that He wants to tell everyone!

This is our immediate future: seeing the joy of our Father as we corporately repent of sins that have held His church back for two thousand years. It is a time to see the ministry of intercession come to full maturity. It is time to see acceptance of the fivefold ministry, especially the prophet and apostle. And it is a time to see the body of Christ come to full maturity and fulfill the Great Commission.

We will see in Nehemiah what God has in store for His fully equipped church: the taking of dominion in all areas of life. God has taken one hundred years to restore His church. He has done painstakingly careful work, with every stone stacked carefully upon another. Every candlestick and every bowl has a specific place. Every Levite and priest has a function. All the gold and silver have been stored there, where they belong. It is now time to take dominion.

The Book of Nehemiah

Chapter 12

The Burden for Jerusalem

In Nehemiah we read:

> In the month of Kislev in the twentieth year, while I was in the citadel of Susa, Hanani, one of my brothers, came from Judah with some other men, and I questioned them about the Jewish remnant that survived the exile, and also about Jerusalem. They said to me, "Those who survived the exile and are back in the province are in great trouble and disgrace. The wall of Jerusalem is broken down, and its gates have been burned with fire."
>
> When I heard these things, I sat down and wept. For some days I mourned and fasted and prayed before the God of heaven.
>
> —Nehemiah 1:1–4

W hen these words were written, we know that the temple had been restored and the second group of Jews had returned to Israel. Ezra had also returned and had brought revival to the Jews in Israel. All of this had already taken place. But Nehemiah had a greater vision than only the restoration of the temple. His heart had been gripped by the desire to see Jerusalem restored. This was a city he had never seen. He had been born in either Babylon or in Persia. He would have been a fairly young man, maybe even a child, when Ezra returned to Israel.

Nehemiah had it ingrained into him that his home was Jerusalem, even though he had never seen it. But why was he so overcome when he heard that the wall of Jerusalem was destroyed? I submit to you that there was something innate inside him that realized the wall of Jerusalem represented the sovereignty of the kingdom of YHWH.

Nehemiah was not a priest or a Levite. He was a government official. I submit to you that Nehemiah is a type of the coming apostolic ministry of the church. In fact, he is a type of the apostolic ministry in the marketplace. What do I mean by this? God is looking to create apostolic ministry to establish the kingdom of God, not in the four walls of the church, but in the middle of what the world has.

For example, Rory and Wendy Alec, a couple from South Africa, have been raised up to bring apostolic anointing to the area of television. Similarly, God has raised up Paul Crouch, Jr. in the area of Christian television and movie production. These people are bringing the apostolic—kingdom building and leadership—to the area of entertainment. These people are not apostles in a traditional sense of the word. They don't seem to be Bible-college graduates, ready to preach and having pulpit ministry. But they are, I assure you, apostolic in their calling and anointing. They are called to establish and set in order the kingdom of God where it hasn't existed before.

The advent of true apostolic ministry in the church as a whole has been absent since the death of the original apostles over nineteen hundred years ago. But since the 1990s, God has begun to raise up apostles all over the body of Christ. As we will see, God's will for this day is to see apostles and prophets in all areas of this world's system. We are on the cusp of a whole new move of God—the move of the church into this world so that "the kingdoms of this world [will become] the kingdom of our Lord and of his Christ" (Rev. 11:15).

Nehemiah received a supernatural burden for the city of Jerusalem. He had not seen it, but he knew that he knew that he had to do something about its sorry state. Just as he felt this overwhelming burden for the city of his people, God is raising up people with specific burdens for their hometowns, their workplaces, their areas of expertise. These are not simply self-willed desires to see these places improved; they are supernatural burdens to see these areas taken for the kingdom of God.

The first wave of this move of God involves this burden in what is coming to be called "marketplace ministry." God has waited for two thousand years to see His church move outside the four walls of its comfort zone and get into the world to take it for His kingdom. We will always need our full-time ministers within the church. They are there to build us up so we can do this work. But this is now a new season. We must understand that God is birthing something so new that it has never occurred in the history of the world: "Forget the former things; do not dwell on the past. See I am doing a new thing! Now it springs up; do you not perceive it? I am making a way in the desert and streams in the wasteland" (Isa. 43:18–19).

The full potential of the church spoken of in Ephesians is to bring the kingdom of God to earth. Jesus taught us to pray, "Let Thy kingdom come on earth as it is in heaven." This is the goal. Jesus is not coming for a defeated church hiding in the corner until He rescues it. He is coming for a glorious church! This church will be found occupying until He comes. An occupying army is one that is present in a land and maintaining control. This is our destiny in His Spirit.

So Nehemiah fasted and mourned for some days. Then he began to pray: "O Lord, God of heaven, the great and awesome God, who keeps his covenant of love with those who love him and obey his commands . . ." (Neh. 1:5).

The first thing Nehemiah did was to worship. He told God how awesome He was and reminded Him of His covenant of love. You know, the first thing is always worship when you come into His presence. In fact, this had to be the first area that God had to restore in order to make the rest of His will on earth occur through His people. Nehemiah worked for the king and would have been one of the king's most trusted servants. He understood the importance of entering the king's presence with a contrite, respectful attitude and demeanor. How much more respect does the great God of heaven, who holds all things together by His words, deserve?

The restoration of worship began about the same time as the restoration of the apostolic ministry. In the 1990s, we began to see restoration of true worship. The worship-music movement began then. In fact, this was the first part of the first wave of restoration in this apostolic era. It was joined shortly after by the restoration of true intercessory prayer on a broad scale. There has always been some worship, just as there has always been some intercession. But there has been a vast shift in the worldwide *ecclesia* within the past ten years to see a whole movement of praise, worship, and intercession, as if the labor pains have grown in intensity and frequency in these last days.

Nehemiah also invoked the covenant. Understanding of covenant relationship and power is also being restored presently. As our understanding of covenant increases, so will our ability to utilize our covenant. We must show to the world that we serve a covenant God, as evidenced by the miraculous.

With that in mind, we see that Nehemiah moved from worship into intercession for his people and his city:

> Let your ear be attentive and your eyes open
> to hear the prayer your servant is praying
> before you day and night for your servants,
> the people of Israel. I confess the sins we
> Israelites, including myself and my father's
> house, have committed against you.
>
> —Nehemiah 1:6

Nehemiah moved into intercession; he began with repentance for his sins and the sins of his people. He identified with this sin, even though he was not alive when the sins that caused the diaspora occurred in the first place. This is an earmark of the heart of intercession. Knowing that sin grieves the heart of God is not enough. *Feeling* grief over sin is the beginning of intercession.

In the church, this was the seed of the prayer movement. In the 1980s, God called a man named Mike Bickle to do something that had never been done before: to start a twenty-four-hour prayer house to prepare the way of the Lord. It has become the International House of Prayer. Thousands of people have been drawn to this movement. Its purpose is to worship God continuously and to intercede for the world and for the church. This prayer/worship/intercession movement continues today. In many ways, it is still in its infancy. But the church is beginning to realize that we must enter into a deeper relationship with the Lord Jesus Christ, and we must first take dominion in the spirit realm before we can take dominion in this earth.

After confession, Nehemiah moved to repentance. He reminded God of the covenant:

> Remember the instructions you gave your servant Moses, saying, "If you are unfaithful, I will scatter you among the nations, but if you return to Me and obey My commands, then . . . I will gather them from there and bring them to the place I have chosen as a dwelling for my Name."
> —Nehemiah 1:9

Intercession must come to the place of pure prayer, invoking the covenant of love that we have with our creator. It is this covenant that gives us the right to ask. In this present time, we are just beginning to realize the depth of the richness of the covenant in Christ that we possess. We must invoke that covenant in the blood of Jesus to see the completion of what has been started. Nehemiah did this and then made his request:

> Give your servant success today by granting him favor in the presence of this man [the king].
> —Nehemiah 1:11

He let his request be made known to God. He was specific in his request. This is the key to successful intercession. James said, "You do not have because you do not ask God" (James 4:2). Once you have worshiped and given God His due honor, once you have moved into confession and purified yourself, once you have invoked the covenant in the blood of Jesus, then it is time to ask specifically for what you need.

Understanding the framework of intercession is where we have come from in the past ten years. We now understand the basic framework. Now God will take us to new depths of intercession. We have moved into a time that we must take dominion in the spirit world so that the name of Jesus may be established as the only name that deserves worship on earth.

After Nehemiah won his battle in the spirit realm, he took action; he went to work, trusting that God was with him. Nehemiah had already been strategically placed by God where he was. But if he had not prayed and wrestled in the spirit realm, he would not have been empowered at his crucial moment. It is not enough to be strategically placed. We must realize that we are where God wants us *and* that we have interceded for that hour that God will use us to change the world around us. This is the essence of dominion.

It was the month of Nissan, the month of the Passover, when Nehemiah's hour came. Perhaps he was thinking about "next year in Jerusalem" as he poured the wine for the king. The king noticed that Nehemiah's usually cheerful countenance was downcast:

> I was very much afraid, but I said to the king, "May the king live forever! Why should my face not look sad when the city where my

fathers are buried lies in ruins, and its gates
have been destroyed by fire?"

—Nehemiah 2:2–3

I've heard it said that courage is not the absence
of fear, but it is action in the face of fear. This is what
Nehemiah had. He was shaking in his boots! But despite
the fear he felt, he spoke boldly, silently praying to God
as he did. And God did the impossible: He turned the
heart of a pagan king toward the man of God.

This is what God is going to do next: the wealth
of the Gentiles will come for the work of God. Does
that seem impossible? Of course it does! But we serve
an incredible God. His desire is to see His people
rule and reign in this world. What is impossible for
man is possible for God. To establish the kingdom
in the world will take financing, favor, and action.
God is not coming for a defeated, sorry, ragtag band
of losers. He's coming for a glorious church without
spot or wrinkle. Our mandate is to occupy until He
comes—not hide until He rescues us.

This move of God to restore wealth will be given
to those who have proven that they will not spend
it upon themselves (we will see this in Nehemiah's
character later). The people who gain the wealth of
the Gentiles will be people who have proven themselves good stewards of God's money. He will not be
giving it to those who have acted foolishly with little,
spending it on big houses and fancy cars. He will
give it to those who have sold all for the kingdom of
God. This wealth is not so Christians can live well. It
is for the great harvest of the lost. This is key.

So many Christians have been foolish with money, from the lowliest new church member to the most famous evangelist. Have you been faithful with little? If you have been faithful to invest in the kingdom, then perhaps God will entrust you with much. But if you have been foolish, running up credit cards, buying houses that are large and lavish, driving cars that make other people jealous, well, perhaps you should take another look at your life.

God is not insisting we live like Mother Teresa. But faithfulness to do what's important to God must be our deepest desire. Having His heart for the lost, for the poor, and for the hungry—this is what He is looking for. When the move of God to transfer wealth into the kingdom comes, He will entrust the funding of His work to the stewards who have been faithful and obedient with little.

The king granted all of Nehemiah's requests. He lacked nothing. The king even provided an army escort (see verse 9). God will sovereignly provide protection from unexpected places for our journey. We will move safely, even though it seems impossible. We will have protection from unexpected places as we move to accomplish dominion in the earth. But we will not be without enemies:

> When Sanballat the Horonite and Tobiah the Ammonite official heard about this, they were very much disturbed that someone had come to promote the welfare of the Israelites.
>
> —Nehemiah 2:10

Those factions that will oppose us will be aware of the favor we have received. They will be angry. But as we start this journey to dominion, they will take no action . . . yet.

I went to Jerusalem, and after staying there three days I set out during the night with a few men. I had not told anyone what my God had put in my heart to do for Jerusalem.
—Nehemiah 2:11–12

The first thing Nehemiah did upon arrival was rest. He took three days to rest. Three is the number of God, representing wholeness and holiness. As we move into this time of restoration of all things, we must first rest in God. We must come to a season of wholeness and holiness. Remember that the one thing in Jerusalem that had been completed at this time was the temple.

The temple is a type of the body of Christ. In this next move of God, all parts of the temple will be restored. The fivefold ministry will be in operation in the whole church. The people of God will move into their areas of ministry all over the body of Christ. Saints will come to the point of understanding where they fit into the body of Christ. They will be called to repentance by "Ezra." There will be a call to holiness all over the church.

Nehemiah represents the apostolic call in the marketplace; in other words, outside the four walls of the church. When Nehemiah waited three days, God was saying that the apostolic call of the market-

place moves only when there is holiness and wholeness first.

Nehemiah began his move at night. He told
no one of his plans but rather chose a few trusted
men to accompany him as he inspected the walls of
Jerusalem. His going was so treacherous that he was
forced to dismount and walk at points along the wall.
He inspected it thoroughly. This represents a time of
going in under the radar for the marketplace apostles. They will have to start with a few trusted people.
They will inspect the "gates" (more on those later).
Then they will make their move.

This move will involve all of society. After the
marketplace apostles have kept counsel with God
alone and have accomplished what must be done in
secret—intercession, planning, and planting—they
will be established in their authority by God, who
has placed them strategically.

Finally, at the right moment, Nehemiah made
his announcement to the leadership of Israel: he
announced his plan to rebuild the walls. Because
Nehemiah prepared, prayed, and fasted, and because
he clearly had the favor of God on him, all the leadership of Israel readily agreed to his plan and began
to build.

It was at this point that the enemies of Israel rose
up and began to both ridicule and threaten Nehemiah:
"What is this you are doing? . . . Are you rebelling
against the king?" (v. 19).

I love Nehemiah's response: "I answered them
by saying, 'The God of heaven will give us success.
We his servants will start rebuilding, but as for you,

you have no share in Jerusalem or any claim or historic right to it' " (v. 20).

Nehemiah's answer is our answer in this hour that is coming. We will unquestionably be attacked verbally. But our God will give us success. We are called to this hour. It is God's kingdom that must be rebuilt, and we will be the ones to do it, not the unbelievers. They only *think* they know the king and what he wants. But we do know Him and exactly what He wants!

This first attack, mockery and ridicule, is what usually happens when the people of God begin to stand up against the ways of the world. The enemy thinks that the use of words to intimidate can stop the people of God. It will be important for us to stand firm in the face of this verbal attack. We can fight words with the Word of God. When we know His Word, especially His *rhema* to us in that hour, we will be able to defeat the enemy.

This first attack is already upon us in this hour. The media and public opinion are turning against us on every front. But we have the Word—*the rhema*— of our God. We already know what His desire is: that we occupy until He comes. We are the head, not the tail. We are to affect every area of life. We are to be salt and light. We have the favor of the King!

The answer we are to give in this hour is to glorify God in the face of the enemy and remind him that he has no part in the kingdom (see verse 20). Note that the enemy cannot stop us but only try to discourage us to stop rebuilding. It is our choice to give in to the mockery and threats or to throw it back at the enemy, give God glory, and continue.

This verbal attack is just the first of many waves of attack. We need to settle in our hearts that we are in a war. We must become war hardened, but not battle weary. Our intimate fellowship with Jesus is what will enable us to do this; we cannot depend on our own power in this. This battle is not ours, but the Lord's.

Chapter 13

The Gates

The gates are representative of every walk of life on earth. You see, God's goal in this is to have His people rebuild every area of society. When I look back at my life, and when I reflect on the lives of many others I've known, I marvel at how God has strategically placed His people in all sorts of unlikely places. There are saints in health care, education, the arts, media, the government, the military, business, and commerce. There are godly families that exemplify His love. There are farmers who have prayed for rain in a drought and brought the rain from heaven to save not only their crops but also the fields of everyone around them. These people of God are not in the wrong place. They have been placed where they are to show the world who God is!

These areas of life are the "gates." As we will see, God has deliberately chosen people to rebuild the gates of life. God is never arbitrary. His plan is deliberate and thorough. We can take comfort in the fact that none of us are where we are for no reason. We are strategically placed for the hour that is coming—the body of Christ taking dominion.

Nehemiah enumerated ten gates to be restored, as well as three towers and a special "house of heroes." What do these gates mean? Why are they important? Who did the work? We are going to attempt to answer these questions. It is in looking at these gates that we will be able to understand where God is going in our immediate future.

Perhaps the most significant theme that we must remember during this restoration of the wall is this: all the restoration took place simultaneously. This was not progressive. This was all at once. All parts of this wall were reconstructed at the same time. As you read of this restoration in Nehemiah, keep this in mind for present-day application. We are not looking at something that will take several generations to accomplish. We are looking at a sovereign move of God that will occur quickly, provided we are willing to fight and build at the same time.

The first gate is the Sheep Gate. It was rebuilt by the high priest and his fellow priests. This gate was used to bring in the sheep used for sacrifice. This is the first area that must be conquered if we are to accomplish what God has for us outside the four walls of the church. The priests rebuilt this gate. Worship is always first. Surrender is always first. Nothing can be accomplished without this. If we do not surrender first and set God above all else, we are not empowered by Him, and all we do is simply wood, hay, and stubble. It will be burned up. This gate represents the area of religion.

When God is first, and when He is worshiped, then He permeates us. He empowers us. He gives us both the vision and the grace to accomplish this vision. Also, God always starts with His spiritual leadership. It is the *priests* who will start this work. There are two groups in the kingdom: there are *kings* and *priests*. The priests must rebuild this area of surrender so that they become examples of true worship to the rest of the people. It is the ministry that must transform the church from a religious entity to a living, breathing organism on fire with passion for Christ.

But the priests didn't stop there. They continued "building as far as the Tower of the Hundred, which they dedicated, and as far as the Tower of Hananel" (Neh. 3:1). The Tower of the Hundred was used to house the king's guard or perhaps the temple guard. This tower represents the execution of the king's edicts to enforce the laws as they are already written. Or to put it more simply, it represents the company of intercessors. You see, intercessors don't make things happen. They declare what is on God's heart. They give voice to God's purposes; they listen to the King then declare what He has told them, thus *executing His orders* in the Spirit.

Soldiers do not make laws. Soldiers *enforce* the laws that are made by the king. This is the function of intercessors. When intercessors pray, they first receive a burden to pray from the Holy Spirit. It is that burden that compels them to pray. This burden to pray, received from the Holy Spirit, is what will bring real change on earth. This is what Scripture says:

> May the praise of God be in their mouths and a double-edged sword in their hands, to inflict vengeance on the nations and punishment on the peoples, to bind their kings with fetters, their nobles with shackles of iron, *to carry out the sentence written against them. This is the glory of all his saints.*
> —Psalm 149:6–9, emphasis added

One translation says, "to execute the *judgment* written" (KJV, emphasis added). You see, it's already written! The work of intercession is to carry out what is already written. We are executing this judgment, not on people, but on the demonic principalities over nations, cities, and people groups. We are doing this to bring about the changes that God has already declared.

So the second piece of the puzzle of God's move is the advent of the worldwide intercessory prayer movement. The Tower of the Hundred is also restored by the leaders of the church. It is within the church that the prayer movement must take place so that the rest of the restoration may take place.

Finally, the priests restored the Tower of Hananel. The word *Hananel* means "grace." Grace is the abiding presence of God that empowers us to be what God wants us to be and do what God has called us to do. Without grace, we can accomplish nothing. It is all about Him. Remember, any work done by us is wood, hay, and stubble. We *require* grace if we are to see restoration come. So after we have worshiped, and after we have found the heart of God and executed His will through prayer, we receive abundant, overwhelming grace to accomplish His will on this earth.

This is what the priests restore. We see these things happening right now in our midst. Anticipate the flood of grace. We are on the verge of seeing a flood of grace like the church has never before experienced. This great outpouring of grace will bring a flood of miraculous, supernatural power for revival—for restoration that the world will have to notice. God's mission is not to just see His church restored. He wants to see the great harvest. But it is all about Him—His power, His way, His timing. He is an extravagant God. He will work in extravagant ways, if we will extravagantly worship and pray.

The next section was restored by the men of Jericho, and after them, Zaccur, son of Imri. They did not work on any gates. But every gate is attached to a wall. The men of Jericho were part of an historic city. This city had been taken through obedience and praise. Praise defeated this strong, walled city, and its walls fell. *Zaccur* means "mindful," and *Imri* means "strong." When we put this together, we find that strength comes through praise. It indicates the coming deeper intimacy that awaits us. This intimacy with the Father—in a depth we have not yet experienced—will give us a new strength to take on the dominion of all areas of society. Again, it is not in our strength that this will be accomplished, but rather it is a new strength we will draw from this intimacy in worship with God.

The Fish Gate was restored by Hassenaah (which means "pointed"). The next section was restored by Meremoth ("heights"), Meshullam ("allied"), and Zadok ("just"). This gate was used to bring in the fish to sell. It represents the world of commerce. Gates always represent authority and dominion. This gate represents the saints taking authority over the world of commerce. This is not something that will be accomplished by our own strength. This is something that must be accomplished by the power of God.

The names of the men who restored are significant as well. Look at their Hebrew meanings: "pointed," "heights," "allied," and "just." *Pointed* indicates focus. Those who are called into the world of business must be focused on their task. It is so easy to be distracted by what the world is saying: that collapse is coming, that we need to fear because financial doom is impending. But God says no. We must focus on what God's Word says: "A sinner's wealth is stored up for the righteous" (Prov. 13:22). The word *heights* indicates where our vision must come from; we must be seated with Christ in heavenly places. We must allow God to take us to the heights so that we may gain His perspective and know when to act in order to succeed in this world. *Allied* indicates how we must join ourselves to others. By becoming joined to other saints in this work, we will see God's will accomplished, that "the kingdoms of this world will become the kingdom of our God, and of His Christ" (see Revelation 11:15). And finally, *just* indicates how we must conduct our business. We read in the King James Version: "A false balance is abomination to the Lord, but a just weight is His delight" (Prov. 11:1).

One other note that must be made is the character of Meremoth, son of Uriah. This was the priest who received all the silver and gold from Ezra when he returned. This was a man who was faithful and could be trusted to account for all of it. His major attribute was trust. What a picture of the man of God who is called into the world of commerce!

This is a picture of God's purpose in the business world. This will happen because He has decreed it. It is for those who have proven themselves in the little things; God gives more to those who are faithful with a little. Is your calling to be an apostle to the business world? Then be faithful with the little you have, and listen. He will guide you, because it is the destiny of the church to take dominion, and maybe you are the one who will be called!

The next section was repaired by the men of Tekoa, and the next gate, the Old Gate, was repaired by Joiada and another, Meshullam. We already know that *Meshullam* means "allied." *Joiada* means "Jehovah-known." This gate is a picture of the restoration of the family.

The men of Tekoa worked without their leaders. This is a picture of fractured families that work toward restoration. They work despite the brokenness of their own families. The absence of the fathers is indicated here. A spirit of pride must first be broken before the family can be fully restored. It was pride that kept the nobles away from this work. They refused to submit themselves to supervisors who, in their view, were beneath them. But regardless of the missing "fathers," the men of Tekoa rose up to build. This represents incredible drive and passion for the work of God in the next generation. They are determined to rebuild the family structure. They are passionate about this restoration.

When we see Joiada, who is "known by God," working with Meshullam, who is "allied," we see a picture of the divine love triangle of marriage in which Jesus is at the apex of this triangle and a man and woman make up the other two angles. As they grow closer to a God who is love, the man and woman grow ever closer together; their alliance grows stronger the more they are known by God. The foundation of the family is the foundation of society. Without this old gate of a firm family, there can be no restoration. It must start with the family, where children can grow in the nurture and admonition of the Lord. It must start with a father, who gives them identity, and a mother, who gives them security. All other relationships and all other work stem from this foundation.

All of us are called to this gate. Only by the power of God can this ancient foundation of the family unit be restored. But take heart. Like the men of Tekoa who worked without their "fathers," this next generation of men will work to restore the family.

Continuing around the wall, in the next group were the men of Gibeon and Mizpah. Gibeon was the place where Solomon sacrificed a thousand animals and sought God for wisdom to rule. *Mizpah* means "watchtower." These two towns were actually under the governor of Trans-Euphrates, not the governor of Israel. In other words, they were under a foreign government. They represent international relations and international government—diplomacy—and the restoration of righteousness to this part of government.

Next came a goldsmith, then a perfumer, who made repairs to the wall. These two men were an artisan and a chemist. It seems odd that they would be working in this area. I asked the Lord about this, and His reply was that the areas of art and science are so intertwined with all areas of life that these areas will build along with all other areas. Art reflects life, and science is the advancement of knowledge and truth. Science is also, in a sense, a confirmation of theory. Science, which has been corrupted by the godless, is supposed to be the search for truth. God is going to restore the purity of science and return it to the search for truth. God is also going to restore art to reflect His glory instead of glorifying sin. It will begin to reflect what He is doing in the earth. But there is also a second meaning we will discuss shortly.

Then came a man named Raphiah ("Jehovah heals"). He also seems out of place. I believe that he appears for several reasons. The first reason is that this man was a city official. We are coming to the area of government, so the obvious reason he is here is that he represents local government. But his name, "Jehovah heals," shows that supernatural healing is also a part of this restoration. While he is not associated with a gate per se, he is significant in that healing will become a part of everyday life. It will become the norm rather than the exception.

There were others, too, who repaired the areas in front of their own homes. A man named Malchijah ("king appointed by God") repaired the Tower of Ovens. Shallum ("recompense") repaired the next section with the help of his daughters. They represent both international commerce (the ovens) and international justice (recompense).

The Valley Gate was repaired by Hanun ("favored") and the men of Zanoah ("rejected"). These two are a picture of justice: the favored and the rejected, the scales on which the judged are balanced. The goldsmith is a picture of tribute; the perfumer, a picture of veneration. Taken together, they speak of government, rulership, and diplomacy.

The Valley Gate, the Tower of Ovens, and the wall leading up to it are a picture of all aspects of government. This gate represents the restoration of godly government and the taking of dominion there. The man who repaired the Tower of Ovens, Malchijah, was a "king appointed by God." The tower itself, which would have been used by the king, is a picture of the care that government is supposed to have for the people it serves. The earthly king thinks only of himself. But in government that is founded on godly principles, the king becomes the servant. What did Jesus say? "If anyone wants to be first, he must be the very last, and the servant of all" (Mark 9:35).

Godly government will be restored, but only through the servant leadership of those wholly given to the lordship of Jesus Christ. First is the King of Kings, who is the "king appointed by God"; then once that is established, all others are servants who rule under Him. What a different concept from the governments we see on earth today!

The Tower of Ovens also represents the refining fire of God. Those who will be called to this area of dominion will face refining fires that will test and try them in order to ready them for the huge leadership calling they have. Leading people is not easy, and leading nations is, well, huge. These leaders will be refined as gold. They will have the fragrance of worship on them. They will be under the authority of the cross and will understand authority and the need for submission to the King of Kings. This is the picture of godly government.

The next gate is the Dung Gate. Interestingly, another man named Malchijah, son of Rechab, ruler of Beth Hakkerem, worked on its restoration. This is another "king appointed by God." There is not much said about this gate in the text, but its purpose seems self-explanatory. As I prayed about the purpose of this gate, I reread the text:

> He rebuilt it and put its doors and bolts and bars in place.
> —Nehemiah 3:14

Perhaps this may sound like reaching, but I felt that this gate actually has two meanings. The first is that it is an extension of government; it represents the military, the strength of bolts and bars for protection. Malchijah is an additional "king," and he is the son of Rechab, which means "rider," as in a cavalry rider.

While there is not much said about this gate, I believe the Lord is saying He will have righteous men in the military. When George Washington was general of the Continental Army, he did not allow a man to swear. He punished any man who took the Lord's name in vain. He held Christian services faithfully. This is a far cry from the "don't ask, don't tell" policy, or even worse policies, that we see in the military today.

I believe that God is going to begin to establish a godly military system again. This gate represents the rebuilding of an army that exemplifies strength, dignity, and honor and that puts Jesus, the commander in chief, at the center of its discipline.

The second meaning of this gate is the more obvious one. This was the gate that people used to dispose of the unclean things. It was used for hygiene, thus it represents health care. In this area, I believe God is going to bring His power to bear, and those called to health care will see opportunities to bring healing in a supernatural way to the sick. Health care has always been about helping, but this will be a supernatural move—doctors and nurses praying for the sick and seeing them healed!

As I pondered the meaning of this gate and its implications for health care, I understood that much of health care—the doctors and nurses—already have compassion and care deeply for people. That is why they became health-care professionals in the first place. What will change is that it will be God's compassion, His caring and His power to heal, on a massive scale. Imagine clearing out hospitals by the power of God! Imagine supernatural words of knowledge to enable a doctor or nurse to give advice that will change a person's life! That is what is coming to health care!

The Fountain Gate was repaired by Shallun ("recompense"), son of Col-Hozeh ("every seer"), of Mizpah ("watchtower"). Nehemiah notes he that he roofed it over. He also repaired the pool of Siloam near the king's garden. From there, another Nehemiah (not the author), the ruler of Beth Zur ("place of the rock"), who was a descendant of Caleb, repaired the wall past the tomb of David and up to the House of the Heroes.

These all speak of vision, fame, and attention. This gate represents the area of media and entertainment. This area, which has all the temptations of fame and glory, is perhaps one of the toughest areas of restoration. As the text indicates, there were many complex areas along this part of the wall. There were stairs, pools, a very famous tomb, and finally the House of the Heroes. This area was the area where building had to be very carefully done to avoid destroying these precious sites. The builders called to restore in this area today are not only going to restore in the existing entertainment and media, but they will also, I believe the Lord is saying, be visionaries who will cut new paths and perhaps even find new avenues of using the media for the glory of God.

The temptation in this area, to take glory for oneself, is a real concern. For those who are called to this area, keeping their relationship with Jesus fresh is imperative. Only in that place where He is king will they be able to really see His glory in media.

The next section of wall was completed by the Levites, who were the praisers and musicians. As we move down the wall, we also read:

> Next to him, Baruch son of Zabbai zealously repaired another section.
>
> —Nehemiah 3:20

Baruch means "praise," and *Zabbai* means "pure." This is pure praise, the restoration of the music world, which is intertwined with worship. I believe that with music as part of the arts and entertainment world, God is restoring it as a pure art and a glorification of Himself. Some of this is already evident. We have seen restoration in this area through the contemporary Christian music business. But I also believe that we have only scratched the surface of what God has in mind.

The Water Gate was the next gate to be repaired, and just as the praisers and musicians repaired the wall before it, so this gate represents taking dominion over the arts, specifically the areas of writing and journalism. We again see the men of Tekoa, who worked without their nobles, helping with this area. This indicates that this movement is not in leadership, but in everyday people who are driven to see God's glory restored in prophetic dance, prophetic music, and prophetic art. It also indicates writing, as the water connotes a flow of words. Purity in journalism, without malice and without prejudice—this is the goal of godly writers.

This gate also represents the washing of the water of the Word. As we will see later, this gate became a focal point in the restoration of the Jews. We would do well to pay attention to the Spirit of God in our words. As we speak, we can bring either reconciliation or rejection. Let us pray that the Lord give us grace in our speech!

The Horse Gate was repaired by the priests, and Zadok repaired next to them. The priests were the teachers of Israel. The name *Zadok* means "to make right." The Horse Gate, then, represents the dominion of education.

Education encompasses more than just the three Rs. It is the socialization of our children. Education in this country has become the indoctrination of our children into the new age, socialistic, one-world philosophy of this corrupt age. Taking education seriously and seeing the body of Christ redeem it is of utmost importance. It requires that parents once again take responsibility for raising their children. But all of us must be sensitive to the fact that our children are our future. What they know and how they understand the world will become the predominant philosophy of the future.

In the culture of Israel, literacy was extremely important. The priests were the most highly educated of all the people of Israel. When a boy reached the age of bar mitzvah, about fourteen years, he earned the right to read and comment upon the Scriptures. All Jewish boys learned to read biblical Hebrew, starting at the age of three years. It was incumbent upon fathers to teach their sons the Torah:

> Do not forget the things your eyes have seen or let them slip from your heart as long as you live. Teach them to your children and to their children after them.
>
> —Deuteronomy 4:9

God's plan includes reclaiming education for His glory. What has happened to education, particularly in America, is the abomination of secular humanism and revisionist history. When the saints bring the Spirit of truth into education, they will transform it into what God has meant it to be.

In Nehemiah 3:29, Shemaiah, son of Shecaniah, repaired the East Gate. He did it by himself. Nothing else is mentioned about this, the most important gate. The names mean "Jah has dwelt," "Jah has heard." This gate is the gate that the Messiah will pass through when He returns. Do you realize how significant this gate is?

Why did Shemaiah, son of Shecaniah, repair it alone? Because he represents the Lord Himself, who will repair this gate without anyone's help. This gate represents the lordship and kingship of Jesus Christ. This is the King's gate. He alone will complete this project. It will not be by any other strength or power, but His alone, because He will not share His glory with another. In this sense, we can say that God will rebuild and restore His church, and He alone will receive glory when His church restores the wall of society. He is Lord. He is sovereign.

Finally, the last stretch of wall and the Inspection Gate were repaired by another "king appointed by Jah," who was a goldsmith, and he was joined by other goldsmiths and merchants. They repaired this section of wall, and the wall was joined once again to the first gate, the Sheep Gate.

I had supposed, as I started this, that the Inspection Gate would be the area of medicine and that it would indicate God's authority over medicine. But I am not so sure now. When I look at the names of those who completed this part of the wall, I see "Jah has favored," "thank offering of Jah," and "blessing of Jah." I don't see anything that indicates medicine, the healing arts, etc.

Hanun, whose name means "to have pity on," indicates the compassionate side of medicine. The gate itself was used to inspect sacrifices for the temple. This indicates, once again, the intimate worship of God—intimate because "Jah has favored and blessed," and worship because it is a "thank offering of Jah." So this process of rebuilding starts with worshiping and honoring God, and it ends with blessing and being blessed by God—a picture of complete intimacy with the King of Kings.

As we enter into this season of restoration of our influence in all of society, please remember something: this is not meant to be a gradual thing! *This will be a simultaneous action in all areas of endeavor.* What we must do is seek God to understand our role in the redemption of society and then go after it.

One other thing we must remember is that as we begin to rebuild, there will be opposition—not just a little opposition, but the unleashing of the armies of hell. Satan does not want us to win. He will do whatever he thinks it will take to discourage us, to stop us, and to render us ineffective. We must stay sharp, be alert, and stay focused on Jesus in order to accomplish this part of God's plan.

We will begin to see Satan's strategies in this next section of the Scripture.

Chapter 14

Opposition

Nehemiah writes:

> When Sanballat heard that we were rebuilding
> the wall, he became angry and was greatly
> incensed.
>
> —Nehemiah 4:1

The enemy seems always ready to react, doesn't he? All it takes is for the people of God to begin to build. As Nehemiah and the people began to build as the king had commissioned them to do, the enemies of the Jews reacted.

The first attack is always verbal scorn, ridicule, and the attempt to discourage through the use of words. Sanballat began by calling the Jews feeble. He continued: "Can they bring the stones back to life from those heaps of rubble—burned as they are?"

(v. 2). His minion, Tobiah, also mocked the Jews, insinuating their building was weak.

Words hurt. The Jews heard them. But Nehemiah did not begin to argue with them. He immediately cried out to God and allowed God to exact revenge. He didn't even try to fight with them. He understood that this restoration belonged to God, so he appealed to the great God of heaven who hears and answers.

Once Nehemiah had given his concerns to God, he didn't fret or worry—he simply went back to work!

> So we rebuilt the wall till all of it reached half its height, for the people worked with all their heart.
>
> —Nehemiah 4:6

When the Spirit moves His church to begin to rebuild dominion in the world, you can pretty much plan on the devil throwing accusations at the saints. In fact, the signs of verbal abuse and mockery are all around us. The media, which at the moment is in the hands of the enemy, continues to ridicule and mock Christians. Christians are always portrayed as idiots, uneducated boobs who know nothing and are disorganized, powerless, and even evil. Does the Scripture not say that in the last days men will call good evil and evil good?

We can expect this from the enemy. It is his usual method of attack. When it happens, our response must be to give it to God. It is God's battle, not ours. We must stick to the business of rebuilding and let our El Shaddai handle the enemy.

Because words could not affect them, thanks to the grace of God covering them, they built the wall to half its height. This rebuilding happened quickly. As this move begins, we will make progress despite the enemy's verbal abuse. In fact, we should rejoice. We must be doing something right! It is our commitment to the cause, to knowing God's purpose, that will cause us to work with all our hearts, and this will cause us to be victorious in the face of opposition.

The next attack of the enemy will come when they see that we are making headway: ". . . that the repairs to Jerusalem's walls had gone ahead and that the gaps were being closed, they were very angry" (v. 7). They began to plot attacks. But the builders were wise. They prayed *and posted a guard.*

The builders began to grow weary. When we build, it's easy for our flesh to grow weary and to look at the great pile of rubble that seems so impossible to overcome. The builders also began to fear the rumors of direct attack from their enemies. They began to listen to the discouraging words of their companions. This discouragement is something that we always face in a great work.

Nehemiah faced this head-on in verse 13:

Therefore I stationed some of the people behind the lowest points of the wall at the exposed places, posting them by families with their swords, spears and bows.

Nehemiah understood that there had come a time when they must work and fight together. Whole families together were ready to fight. They were armed and on their guard. The lowest points of the walls were, of course, the most vulnerable. In terms of the church, these places are where we are still weak. It is up to those who are strong in the Lord to be ready to fight for those who are not yet strong. We are sent in families, and we must be ready to protect the young, the weak, and the defenseless. Our families are the congregations into which God has placed us. We always fight in families. We never fight alone.

We may not even have to fight, but when we show the enemy we have been armed with the armor of God, and we are able and ready to wield that armor, we will have called the enemy's bluff:

> I stood up and said to the nobles, the officials and the rest of the people, "Don't be afraid of them. Remember the Lord, who is great and awesome, and fight for your brothers, your sons and your daughters, your wives and your homes."
> When our enemies heard that we were aware of their plot and *that God had frustrated it,* we all returned to the wall, each to his own work.
> —Nehemiah 4:14–15, emphasis added

Our enemies are ready to see us just roll over and play dead. But when we unify in the love of Christ and protect one another in prayer, intercession, and fellowship, we win! I think it is important at this point to revisit the absolute necessity of being connected in a Bible-believing, truth-teaching, loving church family. In the times that are coming, it will be those relationships, those connections with others who can protect us when we are weak, that will give us victory over the enemy:

> We who are strong ought to bear with the failings of the weak and not to please ourselves.
> —Romans 15:1

There will be dangers. It is not wrong to see and understand the dangers. What is wrong is to despair. God's plan is that those who are adept at wielding the weapons of our warfare are to protect others who are also working. Not everyone will work at the same time. Some will fight, some will work, and some will rest.

I once heard a prophetic word given by a brother in our church. He spoke of each of us as sails on a ship. Not all sails are unfurled at the same time, said God through him. Rather, some are being saved for a later time. Others have been taken down for repair and will eventually replace the sails currently in service when those sails need to be repaired or rested. All the sails are needed, but they are in different places of usefulness.

What an excellent picture of our life in the body of Christ! Sometimes when God is using us in a mighty way, we feel on top of the world. Other times, when times are tough, we feel lower than dust. The fact is, God has seasons for each of us. Sometimes we will be building, sometimes we will be fighting or guarding, and sometimes we will be resting. This will be especially important in this coming season.

Romans 12:3 exhorts us not to think of ourselves more highly than we ought to think. The Amplified Version says each person is "not to have an exaggerated opinion of his own importance, but to rate his ability with sober judgment, each according to the degree of faith apportioned by God to him." In this next move of God, this will be particularly important. We must soberly consider our current condition and learn to rely on our brothers and sisters in the faith; in other words, we must learn unity in place of self-reliance.

For the last several decades, we have been accustomed to a one-man show. This move of God is not about having one man who is the star of the show. This move is about all members of the body of Christ understanding how they fit and where they fit. All are important. While God will always raise up leaders like Nehemiah and Ezra, this restoration move will be about each individual working on his part of the wall and being interconnected with the other parts of this great wall.

> From that day on, half of my men did the work, while the other half were equipped with spears, shields, bows and armor. The officers posted themselves behind *all the people of Judah* who were building the wall. Those who carried materials did their work with one hand and held a weapon in the other,

and each of the builders wore his sword at his
side as he worked.
— Nehemiah 4:16–18, emphasis added

The officers posted behind the people are the fivefold ministry, who are there to enable the entire body
of Christ to do the work of the ministry (Eph. 4:12).
The officers are raised up by God to do this work.
Their task is to train, equip, and bring to completion the consecrated people to do the building until
we reach completion; that is, the unity of the faith in
the knowledge of Christ in maturity. In other words,
when this wall is completed, and all the gates are in
place, then the multitudes may enter the safety of the
gates of the city of God — the body of Christ.

Every one of the builders is equipped for battle
by this time. There will be a season of time when we
will be building with one hand while we are ready
to fight with the other. This state of readiness will
come only if we stay plugged in to the source of all
power — Christ. The sword, the Word of God, must
be kept fresh inside of us. The strength to be battle
ready and to also be building must come from a fresh
relationship with the Spirit of God. This means we
will have to put aside complacency and press on
to know Him. This is not something that is accomplished corporately, but individually. We will be as
strong as our weakest link. Each of us must take time
to learn how to use the sword of the Word. Each of
us must receive rest and nourishment at the feet of
Jesus. It is only in this way that we will be strong
enough to accomplish this next move of God.

Nehemiah kept the man who sounded the trumpet with him. He then declared to the officers and nobles:

> The work is extensive and spread out, and we are widely separated from each other along the wall. Wherever you hear the sound of the trumpet, join us there. Our God will fight for us.
>
> —Nehemiah 4:19–20

Nehemiah represents one of God's generals (the apostolic call) in this passage. The trumpeter represents the prophetic call. Note also that the workers were widely separated. God has no problem with diversity in the body of Christ. We can be widely separated as long as we are working together to build. We all have different families that are building. We build together on different parts of the wall, on different gates, and in different areas. But as long as we build His city, we still work together.

The officers and nobles are those called into leadership who are responsible for different parts of this great wall. Their duty is to listen to the apostolic and prophetic to discern the call of where they must fight. Their duty is to rally the troops to the area under attack.

When that call comes, we will rally to help our brothers under attack. This is what unity in the body of Christ is all about. It's not that we are cookie-cutter shapes robotically behaving exactly the same. Rather, we are diverse, creative, and full of the incredible life that Jesus imparts to us, and we are full of love for one another, ready to lay our lives down for our brothers no matter what part of the wall they are from.

The apostolic and prophetic will work together to look far off and understand what is coming. This is the kind of ministry they are called to: seeing dangers before they hit and rallying the troops for the battle. Respecting and understanding this ministry will help the other ministries work and move more efficiently, like the army of God that we are meant to be. When we begin to understand the need for all five parts of the fivefold ministry, I believe we will stop treating certain individuals like rock stars and begin to enmesh these ministries as cogs of a well-oiled machine.

I have never been in the military, but I've been told that when a man becomes a soldier, he first must stop thinking of just himself and begin to become a part of his platoon so that this group of individuals become a band of brothers. They eat together, sleep in the same room, and spend most of their time together. They learn to get along. They learn the chain of command. They come to respect their commanding officers who have the responsibility of moving them forward in a battle without having any casualties of war. This is a picture of the working of the fivefold ministry and the body of Christ. It is not that somebody is more important than another. It is that God is a God of order and that an army moves well under an orderly chain of command.

> Now you are all the body of Christ, and each
> one of you is a part of it. And in the church
> God has appointed first of all apostles, second
> prophets, third teachers, then workers of
> miracles, also those having gifts of healing,
> those able to help others, those with gifts of
> administration, and those speaking in dif-
> ferent kinds of tongues. Are all apostles? Are
> all prophets? Are all teachers? Do all work
> miracles? Do all have gifts of healing? Do all
> speak in tongues? Do all interpret?
> — 1 Corinthians 12:27–30

A key to this transformation—from individuals
to the Army of God—will be the acceptance of the
presence of all five parts of the fivefold ministry as
enumerated in Ephesians 4:11. Also, we will need
to possess an understanding of the design of God's
administration. This is coming and coming soon. In
some ways, it is upon us now, but there are many
in the body of Christ who are still unaware and still
living in the past. Let us pray that God accomplishes
this part of His plan quickly.

When we have come to this place of unity, it will
bring a new, deeper anointing on the entire body of
Christ. Psalm 133 states:

> How good and pleasant it is when brothers
> live together in unity! It is like the precious
> oil poured on the head, running down on the
> beard, running down on Aaron's beard, down
> upon the collar of his robes.

This is the time that the prayer movement will also reach maturity. In every area of the wall, men worked from sunup to sundown, and guards were posted at night. At no time was the wall deserted. In every part of the wall, men kept vigil and never left the city. They all stayed in Jerusalem and took turns posting the guards:

> Neither I nor my brothers nor my men nor the guards with me took off our clothes; each had his weapon, even when he went for water.
>
> —Nehemiah 4:23

In Scripture, clothing frequently refers to righteousness, praise, and holiness. We are exhorted to put on a garment of praise. The priests were to wear pure linen with no blend of fibers in the presence of God. In Revelation 19:8, we read that "fine linen, bright and clean, was given her [the bride of Christ] to wear." (Fine linen stands for the righteous acts of the saints.)

The armor of God in Ephesians 6:18 is worn specifically for prayer, for doing battle with spiritual forces: "And pray in the Spirit on all occasions with all kinds of prayers and requests." The men at Nehemiah's command never even sheathed their swords. They carried them always, ready for battle.

The battles we must fight are the kind that will take both prayer and action. Knowing the chain of command within our church families and being willing to work with those in the extended family of God to accomplish common goals will be imperative in this next move of God. No one church, for example, will conquer the dragon of abortion. It will take all of us working together to overcome the current culture of death. God may raise up very unlikely people in the apostolic and prophetic to organize us to fight. We must be able to recognize that trumpet call so we can quickly rally. Being sensitive to the small, still voice of God inside us is the way.

Chapter 15

Trouble Inside and Outside

This was a time of famine in Judah. While people were diligently building the wall, families were suffering from famine. The Jews began to complain that they had to borrow money to pay taxes, buy food, and keep living, and their fellow Jews were not only lending money at interest but also selling them into slavery to pay their debts!

This was totally against the Torah's teachings regarding lending—and it was sin in the land. These lenders knew the Torah; they knew they were in opposition to what God had told them, but they were doing it anyway. They were prospering on the backs of their brothers and destroying families out of greed. And the ones who were committing these crimes were the nobles and officials!

Nehemiah called a public meeting when he learned of this abuse. Scripture says he said, "When I heard their outcry and these charges I was very angry. . . . 'You are exacting usury from your own countrymen! . . . Now you are selling your brothers only for them to be sold back to us!' " (Neh. 5:6–8).

He publicly shamed those leaders who were actively sinning. He then demanded they give back everything they had taken and pay back the interest they'd been charging. The nobles and officials agreed to do so, and Nehemiah had them take a public oath before the priests. He then spoke a curse over them:

> I also shook out the folds of my robe and said, "In this way may God shake out of his house and possessions every man who does not keep this promise."
> —Nehemiah 5:13

Nehemiah was appointed governor of Judah, and for the twelve years he served, he led by example. He never took the food allotted to governors (by adding taxes onto the people's tax burden), but rather, he "devoted [himself] to the work on this wall" (v. 16). He also did not acquire land. In addition, out of his own pocket, he provided for the expense of daily food for at least 150 people. And the only favor he asked for was from God:

> Remember me with favor, O my God, for all I have done for these people.
> —Nehemiah 5:19

God is about to do a work of exposure and cleansing among His people. He is going to expose those who through leadership have abused their positions and placed great burdens on the saints. God always starts with His leaders when He begins judgment. This judgment will be about two things: greed and spiritual abuse.

In 1 Peter 4:17, we read, "For it is time for judgment to begin with the family of God." God starts with us because we are His representatives on earth. He is counting on our faithfulness to show the lost who He is. If we manipulate one another, if we are unkind to one another, if we take advantage of one another, how will the world ever see the unconditional, sacrificial love the Father has for the lost?

I believe that God will expose the frauds in His body for who they are. It will be hard to face this. These people will be speechless because they will know what they have done. But the grace and mercy of God is so vast, so deep, that we will see repentance come forth from these people. This change will ultimately give the church an enormous amount of strength against the enemy because the repentance among those in leadership will be so thorough that the enemy will not be able to cast aspersions on the saints.

I believe the key to this transformation will be forgiveness among the injured. Those who have been abused must forgive. This will be the true indicator to the world that the love of God is a supernatural love. It is not conditional—it is sacrificial. Our forgiveness will show this, and the world will be hungry for what we have!

These leaders, once reconciled, will begin to use their own resources to help others. The greed the enemy once used to hold them in bondage will be broken, and they will begin to feed the needy with what they have.

When this great reconciliation begins to occur, the enemy will begin to pour out persecution, but his attempts will fail. By this time, most of the wall of social influence will have been built, but it will not be complete. We will begin to draw strength from our influence in society, but the enemy will still hold political power. This power will be wielded to bring shame and destruction on us. It is in this hour that we must understand and use the truth:

> Sanballat and Geshem sent me this message: "Come let us meet together in one of the villages. . . ." But they were scheming to harm me.
>
> —Nehemiah 6:2

The gifts of the Spirit, discernment and wisdom, will show us the truth. Nehemiah survived because he was as wise as a snake and as harmless as a dove. The enemy will attempt to deceive us. We already see much of that in our culture, but the attacks will be specific and targeted to discredit and destroy us.

The truth is the only thing that will keep us safe. I believe that is why God will bring judgment to His church first before the war of words starts. If we are to win, we must be pure. Any leaven in the lump will be ammunition for the enemy. Purity and truth are our allies:

I sent him this reply: "Nothing like what you are saying is happening; you are just making it up out of your head." They were all trying to frighten us, thinking, "Their hands will get too weak for the work, and it will not be completed."

—Nehemiah 6:8–9

Nehemiah demonstrated wisdom. He called their bluff. He also cried out to God for strength. If we think we can conquer what God has called us to conquer in our own strength, we are greatly mistaken. It is God who girds us with strength and who will make our way perfect.

Finally, there will be false prophets with false words from people we thought we could trust. Without the supernatural gift of discernment, we will be deceived: "I realized that God had not sent him, but that he had prophesied against me because Tobiah and Sanballat had hired him. . . . Remember also the prophetess Noadiah and the rest of the prophets who have been trying to intimidate me" (Neh. 6:12–14).

This prayer also indicates a Jezebel spirit that will come forth to deceive and destroy the church. Remember, these "prophets" were from Jerusalem! It is only by discernment and by prayer that we will know the true from the false. The false can be mixed with truth so that it sounds good. But it is a lie!

Nehemiah didn't try to confront these "prophets." He went to prayer about them. Going to God with every word and waiting on Him will be our protection. Jesus said, "My sheep hear My voice." We must know His voice and understand His ways. In other words, when we know how someone thinks, we know how that person will react in a certain circumstance. If we know God's ways, no voice will deter us from His purposes.

If we will remain pure, and if we will stay close to our Lord, then we will be able to see and discern when dark times come. In fact, we will overcome and prosper, and our enemies will be powerless to stop us!

Chapter 16

The Wall Is Completed

Nehemiah continues:

> So the wall was completed on the twenty-fifth of Elul, in fifty-two days. When all our enemies heard about this, all the surrounding nations were afraid and lost their self-confidence, because they realized that this work had been done with the help of our God.
>
> —Nehemiah 6:15–16

God did this! How could such a great work be done in only fifty-two days? This was not a little garden wall; this was a formidable battlement with towers and gates. There were enemies within and without. Even upon completion, Nehemiah admitted that the nobles of Judah were still in collusion with the enemy. But despite their treachery, the wall was completed in record time. This was a quick work!

Nehemiah then appointed gatekeepers, singers, and Levites. His own brother was appointed as mayor of Jerusalem. Hananiah was appointed commander of the citadel because "he was a man of integrity and feared God more than most men do" (Neh. 7:2).

The gates were only opened at noon and were shut at sundown by the guards, and the guards were appointed so that their own homes were in close proximity to the gates. They would, then, have a vested interest in the security of their respective gates.

The wall, the restoration of the social influence of the church, will be completed in record time. This will be a supernatural work. No man will be able to take credit for this incredible restoration. In fact, it will be a sovereign victory with the entire body of Christ taking part in this restoration. While there will be traitors in our midst, nothing will be able to stop the power of God in the midst of a submitted, unified body of Christ.

When the work is complete—when God's sovereignty has been seen in every walk of life—Christ will establish the apostles of each area of life as guards. These will be people who have established themselves in those areas. In other words, those involved in television will guard the media gate. Those involved in commerce will guard the commerce gate. Each area will be guarded in prayer by those closely involved with it. No defenses will be weak.

It will be that those guarding will be established as men of integrity. It will be those proven in Christ who will be allowed to rule. These people, proven in integrity and powerful in prayer, will be established in rulership.

Once the gates were finished and the city of Jerusalem completed, Nehemiah became concerned because the city was sparsely populated. In his words, "God put it into my heart to assemble the nobles, the officials and the common people for registration by families" (Neh. 7:5). He called for a census; however, it was not just a census, but rather a genealogy.

In this genealogy, he searched the records to verify that the priests had the lineage required to serve in the temple. Those who did not have the lineage could not serve and were excluded.

This indicates yet another cleansing by God. He will not allow ministers who cannot "prove their lineage." Those who are going to serve in the great harvest must truly be servants of Christ. Anyone who is not totally committed to Jesus will be excluded. This cleansing will be, I believe, by God; He will separate those who are not truly committed from those who are, because He alone can see a person's heart.

In addition, there will be a great financial blessing into the kingdom of God to make ready the work that is coming next. Those who are "nobles," who have been raised up in the marketplace, will freely give what God gives them. They will recognize that their prosperity is meant for the furthering of the gospel, not for themselves. They will finance the coming harvest.

This will be the final puzzle piece needed to accomplish God's purpose. Once financing is in place, the great harvest will begin. At this point, people will leave "Jerusalem" and go to share the good news:

> The priests, the Levites, the gatekeepers, the singers and the temple servants, along with certain of the people and the rest of the Israelites, settled in their own towns.
>
> —Nehemiah 7:73

These people will be sent out to their own locations. It will be their witness to the world that will bring this great harvest.

Chapter 17

The Great Harvest

The seventh month arrived. This was the month of the Feast of Trumpets, of Yom Kippur, and of the Feast of Tabernacles. This is the holiest month of the Jewish calendar. All of Israel came to Jerusalem:

> All the people assembled as one man in the square before the Water Gate. They told Ezra the scribe to bring out the Book of the Law of Moses, which the Lord had commanded for Israel.
>
> So on the first day of the seventh month Ezra the priest brought the Law before the assembly, which was made up of men and women and all who were able to understand. He read it aloud from daybreak till noon as he faced the square before the Water Gate in the presence of the men, women and others

who could understand. All the people listened attentively to the Book of the Law. . . .

Ezra opened the book. . . . Ezra praised the Lord, the great God; and all the people lifted their hands and responded, "Amen! Amen!" Then they bowed down and worshiped the Lord with their faces to the ground.

—Nehemiah 8:1–6

There is so much in this passage. Bear with me as I explain it piece by piece. First, in the first verse, we read that "all the people assembled as one man." This is an indicator that all people groups will be touched, particularly the Jews:

For He Himself is our peace, who has *made the two one* and destroyed the barrier, the dividing wall.

—Ephesians 2:14, emphasis added

What is Paul talking about here? He is talking about the fact that Jesus pulled down the division between Jews and Gentiles "to create in Himself *one new man* out of the two" (Eph. 2:15, emphasis added). When the people meet as *one man* in this "New Jerusalem,"—this city that is being rebuilt by the Spirit. Jew and Gentile together will form one new man in Messiah Jesus. Thus there will be at this time an ingathering of the Jews during this great harvest. Jews and Gentiles will meet in the kingdom as one man!

They met at the Water Gate, indicating the washing of the water by the Word. These people *asked* for Ezra to read the Torah to them. Their hunger was so great that they could not wait for it. Imagine the shofar blast that called the multitude into fellowship. They must have eagerly run to the temple and begged for the Word of God to be read to them. This is a pastor's dream come true. Such a hunger will be in these new believers that they will be pulling ministry out of their pastors!

This assembly was made up of men, women, and children, but not babies. Such will be the maturity rate of these believers. They will not remain babies but will quickly gain understanding in the things of God. There will be no difference between men and women: "Neither Jew nor Greek, slave nor free, male nor female, for you are all one in Christ" (Gal. 3:28). It will be all who are able to understand, with no respect to persons.

These people listened from daybreak until noon, approximately six hours. The people all listened intently. I'd like to ask anyone I know (including myself) if he or she would stand and listen intently to the reading of the Torah for six straight hours in the hot sun! But such was their hunger. And such will be the hunger of those entering the kingdom in the great harvest.

As soon as the Torah was opened, all the people worshiped, starting with Ezra, the priest. Their respect for every word was so great and their hunger so deep that they were overcome with love for God. This heart is the heart that God will put in these believers.

The Levites continued to instruct the people, explaining the passages they were hearing, "making it clear and giving the meaning so that the people could understand what was being read" (Neh. 8:8). There will be many capable teachers during this time. And people will drink in the teaching and the Word. What a joy to be a teacher of the Word at this time!

This is the season of Yom Kippur, a time of repentance and reconciliation with God. What a perfect picture of the repentance and transformation that the gospel brings! They were in the temple for Yom Kippur, and their city was now rebuilt. They were in repentance, and the people began to weep as they heard the Torah taught to them. This would seem appropriate for those circumstances. But Nehemiah, Ezra, and the priests all stood up and declared:

> "Do not mourn or weep." For all the people had been weeping as they listened to the words of the Law. Nehemiah said, "Go and enjoy choice food and sweet drinks and send some to those who have nothing prepared. This day is sacred to our Lord. Do not grieve, for the joy of the Lord is your strength."
> —Nehemiah 8:9–11

Why would Nehemiah tell the people not to grieve on the day of repentance? Because this was a foreshadowing of what God is about to do in these last days! These people will hear the Word, repent, and rejoice in the incredible gift of salvation that Jesus Christ has purchased for them. Truly the joy of the Lord will be their strength. This will be the complete fulfillment of Yom Kippur and will be the great assembly of people who realize their reconciliation with God has been completed in Jesus. And a great portion will be Jews!

The scales will fall from the Jews' eyes:

> Then all the people went away to eat and drink, to send portions of food and to celebrate with great joy, because they now *understood the words* that had been made known to them.
>
> —Nehemiah 8:12, emphasis added

Compare this with what Zechariah saw only a few years before:

> And I will pour out on the house of David and the inhabitants of Jerusalem a spirit of grace and supplication. They will look on me, the one they have pierced, and they will mourn for him as one mourns for an only child, and grieve bitterly for him as one grieves for a firstborn son. . . . On that day a fountain will be opened to the house of David and the inhabitants of Jerusalem, to cleanse them from sin and impurity.
>
> —Zechariah 12:10; 13:1

Can you see it? They will suddenly see and understand. Oh, for that day to come! What overwhelming joy in both heaven and earth! This moment will be the day the Lord tabernacles with the Jews again. As the next few verses in Nehemiah say, the Jews will see in the Torah the Feast of Tabernacles fulfilled. What a joy!

In Nehemiah 8:16, we read that they built booths all over Jerusalem, but especially in the squares near the Water Gate and the Ephraim Gate. The Ephraim Gate represents the Gentile church. The Water Gate represents the Word coming to Israel again. This will be the greatest revival in the history of the world—the presence of God among both Jew and Gentile, the *one new man!*

And day by day during this time, they will meet together for the public reading of the Word of God until the day of the great assembly:

> On the twenty-fourth day of the same month, the Israelites gathered together, fasting and wearing sackcloth. . . . Those of Israelite descent had separated themselves from all foreigners. . . . They . . . confessed their sins . . . and read from the Book of the Law . . . and spent another quarter [of the day] in confession and in worshiping the Lord their God.
>
> —Nehemiah 9:1–3

This was about two years after the first wave of repentance mentioned in Ezra. Those who had repented of their compromise were now in the temple, weeping and praying, worshiping and interceding. The leaders who had purified themselves are named first. Then all the people who were there worshiped God, recounting His acts, His mercy, His compassion, and His covenant.

Then all the Levites, priests, and leaders took a written oath, affixing their seals to it. Their intention was to keep all the Law and never again neglect the house of God or the city of God. Those who "separated themselves from the neighboring peoples for the sake of the Law of God, together with their wives and all their sons and daughters who [were] able to understand," also joined into the oath (Neh. 10:28).

This season of the church will be a time of full maturing of the prayer, praise, worship, and holiness movements. This season will show to the earth for the first time the mature, complete body of Christ. This season, coincidentally, was exactly 3½ weeks after the completion of the wall, when Ezra stood up on Rosh Hashanah and spoke from the Torah on the first day of the month (see Neh. 8:1). Could it be that the 3½ weeks coincide with 3½ years? It could, of course, just be coincidence, but God never makes mistakes.

We have not spoken about the circumstances that could be present in the world during this time of restoration. We haven't because if we are moving and living and working in the kingdom of God, the circumstances on the earth are immaterial to what God will do. I think the importance of remaining in Him, connected to Him, drawing strength from Him so that He alone receives the glory from whatever we do, is really the central point. This restoration will not be because of the work of our hands. He may use our hands, so to speak. But this is all about the King, not us — His restoration, His timing, His glory.

Chapter 18

The Age of the Nazirite

The word *Nazirite* is an interesting one. Its root is *nazar,* meaning "branch." It can also be understood to mean "separated from," as one who separates himself from drinking wine or who perhaps separates himself from certain other people groups. The Torah speaks of the Nazirite vow:

> If a man or woman wants to make a special vow, a vow of separation to the Lord as a Nazirite, he must abstain from wine and other fermented drink. . . . He must not drink grape juice or eat grapes or raisins. As long as he is a Nazirite, he must not eat anything that comes from the grapevine. . . . No razor may be used on his head. He must be holy until the period of his separation to the Lord is over. . . . Throughout the period of his separation . . . he must not go near a dead body. . . .

Throughout the period of his separation he is consecrated to the Lord.

—Numbers 6:1–8

When the Torah was written, the Jews took this type of vow, but theirs was a temporary vow. Most took such a vow for a given period of time, although a very few lived it for a lifetime. They separated from certain activities and foods and consecrated themselves to the Lord. Sampson was a Nazirite. He never cut his hair. Sampson was separated from things, but his heart was never given to the Lord.

When Nehemiah began to present the Jews with consecration, he meant it to be a permanent vow. The people understood that when they placed their seal on this vow, they were dedicating their lives to the cause of the kingdom of God. They were telling God they would be faithful. Nehemiah, chapters 10 and 11, spells out in detail the cost of this commitment:

All these now join their brothers the nobles . . . to follow the Law of God given through Moses . . . and to obey carefully all the commands, regulations and decrees of the Lord our Lord.

—Nehemiah 10:29

In the ancient world, a covenant was an unbreakable vow between two parties. When a man took such an oath, he knew it could cost him his life if he broke it. No such contract was entered lightly. In our modern world, we really have no such contract.

Not even marriage is held in high esteem anymore. But these people knew what they were doing. They were entering into the covenant, not only for themselves, but also for their families and for generations to come.

This kind of commitment, entering a covenant, is what the Nazirite vow was about. Nothing could break that vow. It was essentially a marriage contract between a person and God. Divorce was not an option. The vow was permanent. It cost everything.

Note that in the Nazirite vow of the Torah, a man could not even break the vow in order to bury a family member. Compare that to what Jesus said:

> Anyone who loves his father or mother more than me is not worthy of me; anyone who loves his son or daughter more than me is not worthy of me; and anyone who does not take his cross and follow me is not worthy of me. Whoever finds his life will lose it, and whoever loses his life for my sake will find it.
> —Matthew 10:37–39

And, again:

> But the man replied, "Lord first let me go and bury my father."
> Jesus said to him, "Let the dead bury their own dead, but you go and proclaim the kingdom of God."
> —Luke 9:59–60

Was Jesus so cold that He didn't care about the feelings of those with families? No! He was referring to the Nazirite vow! Here He was, Jesus of Nazareth (again the root *nazar*), who was also called by Isaiah, the righteous branch (*nazar*). He was talking to Jews, who were familiar with the Nazirite vow since they heard the Torah read to them every week. He was saying to them, "If you walk with Me, you will be like Me, a Nazirite in your heart—separated to YHWH."

With all this in mind, let's look at the Nazirite movement. God is calling us to a higher calling. We are to be in the world, but not of the world—separated *from* the distractions of this world and separated *to* God. The call and commitment of the Nazirite may require radical things in this life, such as not having the Internet if it is a temptation or getting rid of cable television if it is a distraction. This is the call of the Nazirite in our day.

This call is currently being sent forth by God into this generation. It is radical. It is extreme. This means not doing what the world does. It means possible rejection by many. But the consecration means a depth and richness of relationship with Jesus that will make us offshoots of His branch. It means showing the world the face of Jesus as He remakes us into His image.

In Nehemiah, we see that the first one to place his seal of commitment was Nehemiah himself, followed by the leaders (non-priests) of the people. After those in leadership in the secular arena, the Levites, some other leaders, and finally the people signed this vow. It will be in these coming days that those in secular leadership in the kingdom of God will take leadership roles in this new holiness, Nazirite movement.

In Nehemiah 11, we also see that lots were chosen to repopulate Jerusalem. This choice was not left up to individuals. If your lot was chosen, you moved in. Some volunteered to live there, but all were willing to do it. This shows a heart of commitment to the things of God.

Those who choose to "live in Jerusalem" will be called to an even higher level of commitment. They will lay down their lives to go where God calls. It may be some of the unlikeliest people—not great leaders, but simply those who are willing to go. They will find themselves in the presence of the priests and Levites, the temple servants, and many in ministry, although their high calling will still be in the marketplace. They will become leaders only because of their willingness to lay their lives down for the kingdom.

Living in Jerusalem meant you were not farming your land. You had to depend on the largess of others for food. It meant settling in a place that was not home. It was a sacrifice. This heart of sacrifice—of taking up our crosses and following Him—will be the hallmark of the Nazirite in our time.

I think of those who have chosen a missionary's life as being examples of the Nazirite. They have given up home, family, and comfort to live in a place of unfamiliar languages and customs to show the love of Jesus to a lost world. I also think of those who smuggle Bibles into dangerous territories; their sacrifice may mean death. But as the days grow darker, we will all face the Nazirite call. Christ is calling all of us to this. Without this, the body of Christ will remain fragmented and selfish. With this call, this generation will show His light—and change the world.

Chapter 19

The Final Reforms

In chapter 12 of Nehemiah's book, we see a flashback to the time of Zerubabbel. Nehemiah recorded the names of those who served in the temple. He enumerated their lineage, paying respect to those who faithfully served in the temple; that is, the priests, the praisers, and the gatekeepers. In this way, he paid them respect for their faithfulness. In our context, I believe this is where we stop to pay our respect to all of those who built the foundation for the greatest revival in history—the total restoration of God's *ecclesia* on this earth.

But more than that, this is where God will unite all of His church as one. Those who built the foundation will not only be included but will also be honored for their contribution to the restoration of the church:

At the dedication of the wall of Jerusalem, the Levites were sought out from where they lived and were brought to Jerusalem to celebrate joyfully the dedications with songs of thanksgiving and with music. . . . The singers also were brought together from the regions around Jerusalem. . . . When the priests and Levites had purified themselves . . . they purified the people, the gates and the wall.

—Nehemiah 12:27–30

All of the saints will come together and be purified together. Then the whole wall and the gates will also be purified. The whole church will come into the place of purity—the Nazirite vow! No longer will there be divisions of denominationalism, but rather we will recognize all who truly call on the name of the Lord, regardless of label, and we will come into that place of sanctification where Jesus is truly Lord of us all. When this happens and we come to a place of worship in purity, then it will be like it was in Nehemiah's day:

The sound of rejoicing in Jerusalem could be heard far away.

—Nehemiah 12:43

The whole world will hear this sound! In verses 40–42, we read that choirs took their places and sang under the direction of Jezrahiah. His name means "Jah will shine."

It is in this hour that the light of God will be seen in His church because of the unity we will have. In Isaiah 60:1–3, we read:

> Arise, shine, for your light has come,
> And the glory of [YHWH] rises upon you.
> See darkness covers the earth
> And thick darkness is over the peoples,
> But [YHWH] rises upon you
> And his glory appears over you.
> Nations will come to your light,
> And kings to the brightness of your rising.

In this hour, we will see this Scripture fulfilled. Notice that it says there will be deep darkness on this earth. This will not be a pleasant time on the earth, but God is going to do such a work in this hour in His people that He will receive glory, and the nations will see it!

During the dedication of the wall, the Torah was again read, and it was found that no Ammonite or Moabite was to enter the temple. One of the priests had allowed an Ammonite leader (a relative) to have a room in the temple. Nehemiah became angry when he returned from Susa; he rebuked the priests and stripped the guilty priest of his responsibilities.

He also discovered the priests were not taking care of their brothers, the Levites, by providing their portions of the tithes to them. This meant their brothers were starving. Finally, he discovered the Sabbath being profaned by people doing business, even with foreigners, during this sacred day.

He also reassigned the priests and Levites so that faithful men would take care of the Levites, and he assigned guards to keep the gates shut on the Sabbath. Both of these things indicate the seriousness of the commitment to purity and integrity in the coming days and that apostolic vigilance will be necessary.

We cannot compromise, even in little areas. In our businesses, we must stay committed to our fellowship on the Lord's Day. We cannot allow compromise to creep in that will allow "foreigners" through our gates. We must guard our gates. A little leaven leavens the whole lump. This vigilance is crucial if we are to see the great harvest through.

In the last portion of this book, we see again men who married women of Ammon and Moab. Remember that these were the two tribes not allowed into the temple. I believe this speaks to the coming, corrupt, one-world religion. It will be easy to be misled into this religion, because it will be a counterfeit. It will look like the real thing in many ways. A good counterfeit always does. But it will corrupt some of the children:

> Half of their children spoke the language of Ashdod or the language of one of the other peoples, and did not know how to speak the language of Judah.
>
> —Nehemiah 13:24

It will be imperative to stay pure—to know the Word and have a close relationship with Jesus and with His people—in these coming days. If we know the Word and continue to teach it to the next generation, there will be no deception in the generation after this one. But it is up to us.

But there will still be apostasy: "One of the sons of Joiada bar Eliashib the high priest was son-in-law to Sanballat. . . . And I drove him away from me" (Neh. 13:28).

Sanballat represents Satan. The *priest* had compromised so much that he married into the devil's family! This is the kind of apostasy we are facing. And it will be so deceptive. Scripture calls some of the deceptions "signs and lying wonders" (1 Thess. 2:9, KJV). Unless we stay plugged in, we will be exposed to this and fall.

This last warning to us must be heeded. God's plan to do such a great work in this hour comes with a price—our total commitment to Him. If He is Lord of all of us, then we have nothing to fear. It is time to count the cost of following Him. Paying that cost may seem extreme. But the rewards of following Him and knowing Him are so much greater than anything we can even imagine.

Chapter 20

So What Do We Do?

Just as the woman giving birth must go through transition, so are we preparing to give birth to the next move of God. The body of Christ is going through changes—changes that will cull the goats from the sheep in many ways. It is up to each of us to decide where we want to be and which group we want to choose.

Not only do we need to understand the great preparation God has made so that we may be victorious in this season, but we must also begin to ask Him where we belong as we rebuild this wall. Are we part of the fivefold ministry? Are we called to marketplace ministry? What preparation do we need in order to establish the kingdom of God where we are called?

I submit to you that in the past we have been told that if we love Jesus, we need to be in the ministry. But that is only one gate of ten. And there is an entire wall to build! We cannot hide anymore inside the walls of the church. We need to get out into the world.

Recently a young woman came to me and asked if she was wrong to consider a career in law enforcement. Her friends had chided her because she was considering something so "worldly." She was in tears. What came out of me was, I believe, an encouragement from God: "You have delighted yourself in Me. I have put that desire in you."

We must stop thinking that all young people who love God must be ministers. God is calling us to retake the society for Him. It is time to get behind these young people and disciple them in the ways of God so they can have the strength of spirit and character to take Christ to a lost and dying world. They need us to help them get out there.

We also need to impart a fervent, flaming love for Christ to the saints around us. We will see ourselves rekindled as we get on our knees and seek God with all our hearts. This is an hour for passion. This is also an hour for seeking God for a plan for each of our lives, a plan that will take Christ to the marketplace and get Him out of the four walls of the church.

Begin to seek God now for where He wants you and where He wants your children. Begin to instill in the next generation the vision of the rebuilding of the wall. Show singleness of vision; keep your eyes on Jesus. And ask the Lord to show you the fivefold ministry around you. You have an integral part in the building of this wall. We all do.

This is a time of great decision in the church. Will you be a part? Yes, it means giving your all to the kingdom of God. But the rewards of seeing the kingdom come to earth as it is in heaven are, well, priceless.

The time to count the cost is now. If you are willing to be a part of the building of the great wall, then pray this prayer (and mean it!):

Dear Father,

I know that You have a great future for me in the end-time army of God. I have counted the cost, and I lay all I am and all I have at Your feet. I do this because I love and trust You. Show me Your ways, Lord. Teach me Your paths. I will learn Your voice and obey it, no matter what the cost. Please direct me to the part of this wall You would have me build. I will be faithful because You are faithful. I ask You for the grace to accomplish my part of Your plan. In the name of Jesus and for His glory, I pray. Amen.

LaVergne, TN USA
25 June 2010
187423LV00002B/1/P